RESILIENCE
TURNING PERSECUTION INTO PURPOSE

BY DURETI (MIMI) TADESSE

Copyright © 2024 Dureti (Mimi) Tadesse

All rights reserved. No part of this publication may be reproduced, distributed, or transmitted in any form or by any means, including photocopying, recording, or other electronic or mechanical methods, without the prior written permission of the publisher, except in the case of brief quotations embodied in critical reviews and certain other noncommercial uses permitted by copyright law.

*Published by Hemingway Publishers
Cover design by Hemingway Publishers
ISBN: Printed in the United States*

TABLE OF CONTENTS

Dedication v

Acknowledgment vii

About the Author viii

Chapter 1 Introduction 2

Chapter 2 The Nature of Persecution 20

Chapter 3 Personal Transformation and the Trials of Persecution 40

Chapter 4 Community Resilience 60

Chapter 5 Empowering Others 70

Chapter 6 From Local Heroes to Global Advocates 94

Chapter 7 The Final Step 106

Dedication

I give all glory to my Lord, my rock, and Heavenly Father, who has made me complete in Jesus Christ.

To my mother, Atsede Firrissa: thank you for planting the seeds of faith and love for Jesus in my heart. Your prayers, resilience, and lessons in honesty, determination, and generosity have shaped who I am today. I love you deeply, Mom (Astdu koo).

To my late grandmother, Cawwaaqee Guuttatta: your unconditional love, generosity, sacrifice, and wisdom through storytelling nurtured my mind and spirit. You taught me to value authenticity over superficiality. I miss you and love you, Akoo koo.

To my husband, Daniel Daffa (Danny): thank you for your unwavering courage in standing for truth and freedom, even through a decade of imprisonment. Your strength inspires me every day.

To my late uncle, Gebeyehou Firrisa, who stood against corruption and whose life was cut short, and my late cousin, Kulani Mekonen (Kulee Koo), whose struggles remain a symbol of resilience for countless women enduring abuse—you are forever in my heart. To all who fight for justice or feel trapped in pain, you are seen, loved, and capable of greatness.

To Mitike Belina, who gave us our precious Idoshe: thank you for your ultimate sacrifice. I pray your soul rests in peace.

This dedication extends to all who have loved, supported, and inspired me. May your stories, sacrifices, and dreams continue to light the way.

Acknowledgment

I extend my deepest gratitude to my husband, Daniel Daffa (Danny), co-founder of CGWE, for his unwavering encouragement, generosity, and creativity. Your support means the world to me.

To my beloved siblings, children, nieces, nephews, cousins, and extended family—thank you for your prayers, love, and support. I treasure our shared memories and look forward to creating more together.

To the Nekemte Muluwongel Church leaders and members, especially Preacher Beyene Gudeta, Tadesse Bedhasa, and Alemayo Gudeta—thank you for your support during the Derg regime's persecution.

A special thanks to my uncle, Dr. Mekonen Firrissa, for stepping up during my Ma'eklawi prison ordeal and coordinating with my sister Million and Uncle Tolesa. Your presence meant so much.

Gratitude to Negeri Fayisa, Dr. Dima Nogo, late Uncle Teklu Jaleta, and the American Embassy counselor for facilitating my immigration to the U.S.

Thank you to Shanna Huber and Michal Hogan who encouraged me to share my story.

About the Author

Born and raised in Oromia, Ethiopia, Mimi endured for her ethnic background, religious values and gender discrimination, imprisonment, and torture. After seeking asylum in the U.S. in the 1990s, she and her husband found freedom and new opportunities. Mimi pursued education, earning degrees in Business Administration, and built a successful career. With over 23+ years of voluntary nonprofit experience, she is the founder of C.G. Women's Empowerment (CGWE), a Christian based organization dedicated to creating economic self-sufficiency for women, children, and entire villages in Ethiopia's Oromia State

Chapter 1
Introduction

Section I: The Phoenix:

"Only from the ashes of who we were can we rise up to become who we're meant to be."

-Anonymous

There is a mysterious tale of a mythical and mystical bird - an incredible bird, golden as the sun with feathers as red as fire. It is said this magical bird could live for hundreds of years; when it was old, it would erupt in fire and burn to ashes. Then, as if miraculously, a new, young Phoenix would rise in the shadow of the ashes of destruction.

J.R.R. Tolkien said, *"From the ashes, a fire shall be woken, a light from the shadows shall spring."*

The legend of the Phoenix is told in many cultures, and many names know this amazing bird. Its story embodies facing challenges with strength and the resilience to rise to rebirth in the face of overwhelming adversity.

The lesson of resilience from the Phoenix myth is powerful. I have learned this lesson of resilience the hard way. Life brings challenges and immense setbacks, just like the flames hungry to scorch and burn the Phoenix. However, the power of the Phoenix's story is not the destruction it faces but how it rises in the face of destruction. How it bravely faces the flames. The Phoenix's determination teaches us that no matter the severity of the adversity, there is always potential for renewal and growth.

The Phoenix's story of resilience reminds us that life never stops. Every challenge life throws our way might be an opportunity to recognize our own inner resilience, potential strength, and what we are capable of doing and withstanding.

As Helen Keller wisely said, *"Although the world is full of suffering, it is also full of the overcoming of it."*

Each rebirth of the Phoenix symbolizes a transformation—emerging stronger and more beautiful from the trials of fire. In human experience, our trials, failures, and difficult experiences can lead to personal growth and wisdom. The Phoenix encourages us to view these experiences not as final defeats but as transformative processes that refine our character and spirit.

Therefore, just like the bird that rises from its ashes, so can we! This legendary creature is not just a story from the past but a continuous source of motivation that deeply connects with human experience. As the American poet Maya Angelou once said, *"We may encounter many defeats, but we must not be defeated."* Like the Phoenix, let us accept the flames of our challenges and rise stronger!

Section II: Author's Journey

Now, if you are wondering why I am talking about the Phoenix so much, let me tell you that my story is also filled with trials and rebirths that mirror this legendary bird's journey.

Just like the mythical bird, I have faced numerous challenges and moments of devastation. Life has thrown its fiercest fires at me, trying to consume my spirit and break me down. But each time, from the ashes of defeat, I found a way to rise. This is not just a story of survival but a story of resilience and transformation. I'm pretty sure your eyes will widen, and you won't be able to stop turning the pages because, yes, these trials were the reality of my life.

The story starts at Jal Meda Sports Ground in the Finfinnee (Addis Ababa) 6-kilo area. Finfinnee is the capital city of the state of Oromia, in Ethiopia. Finfinnee, or as you might know it, Addis Ababa, is a city full of life and noise, and that's where I was born, right in the heart of it.

I was born into a family of six children, with me being the third. Imagine our home, continually noisy, always something going on. My parents and my eldest sister's early years were a whirlwind of moves. They didn't stay put in one place for long because of my dad's job. First, they moved from Finfinnee to Wollaga, specifically Yubdo City, where Dad worked as a pharmacist for the Ethiopian government. Here, my second eldest sister came into the world. They didn't stay there long and were soon back in Finfinnee. That's how it was: constant moving and endless chaos.

RESILIENCE

After moving back, dad continued working for the government. This time he worked at the Ethiopia Public Health Tuberculosis Care Center in the Merkato market, close to the Former bus station. Things might have felt like they were settling down. But life has a way of throwing surprises, and soon, Dad got the fantastic idea of opening a pharmacy. Here we were packing up yet again, this time to a place near Gimbi called Gu'i in Haru Woreda.

My mother, Atsede Firressa and my father, Tadesse Dheressa

This time, my Mom (Atsede Firrissa) took a brave step and refused to move with my dad. She had enough and refused to stand for his abusive behavior any longer.

Those early days after their separation were busy days. My grandma, Cawwaaqee Guuttatta, came to live with us to help our family after I was born. She was a huge help to my mom. Eventually, she took us and returned to her farm, where she grew coffee and corn. Our life in Nekemte started after that.

Left to right - my oldest sister Serawit, Me (Mimi) and my older sister Million in Finfinne (Addis Ababa)

Nekemte was the place where both my parents were born and raised. It was a good place, but not everything was perfect. Dad... well, he started a new family without telling us. During that same time my mother had three of my younger siblings. My Dad stayed with her only for intimate reasons. He was abusive and untrustworthy.

As I write this, I ponder how it feels when your family splits up! Just a regular day in paradise, right? You wake up one morning, and boom, your family picture looks nothing like the one hanging on the wall. It was a difficult time for our family, especially when we found out about his second wife. My mom couldn't stand it any longer. She was done with his abuse and with the discovery of his second wife she decided it was time for a divorce. It was then we moved in with my grandmother.

Meanwhile, the government policies at the time only made things worse. The government was seizing lands of the Oromo people, including my grandmother's farm, leaving many families like ours struggling. This was my first taste of persecution, though I didn't fully understand it then. It was only later that I realized we were being targeted, not just because of my father's actions but also because of our Oromo heritage.

Being Oromo in Ethiopia meant facing discrimination at every turn. The Oromo people, despite being one of the largest ethnic groups in the state of Oromia, have long been marginalized. Their oppression goes back to when the the Abyssinians forcefully occupied our land and repressed our people in the late 1880s. Our language was suppressed, and our cultural identity was and still is often attacked. My legal name, Dureti, was a clear marker of my Oromo identity, and I faced ridicule because of it.

Map of Oromia

When I was in Black Lion High School in Finfinnee (Addi Ababa), living with my sister at the time, other students would tease me and mock my Oromo name. It got so bad that I asked my parents if I could change it. But my family stood by me, telling me my name was beautiful and meaningful. They empowered me to stand up for myself and be proud of who I am. Thanks to their support, I learned to love my name, Dureti, and to accept my identity as an Oromo in Oromia, where Jesus placed me.

RESILIENCE

When I was in Black Lion High School in Finfinne (Addis Ababa)

In 1977, life threw another surprise our way and we lost my uncle. I still remember how one of my grandmother's nieces, Asfaw Idosa, came to our house and knocked on the gate early in the morning, around 4 am.. My grandmother and mom were startled and got up quickly. They thought it was the usual government harassment. But this time, it was different.

"It's me, Asfaw. Your son Gebeyehou is seriously sick. You need to get up, get dressed, and go to Addis Ababa now," she said. Addis Ababa (Finfinnee) was 335 km away from where we lived in Nekemte. Can you imagine their panic?

DURETI (MIMI) TADESSE

My mom and grandmother dressed quickly, packed a few things and asked some family members to stay with me and my siblings while they were gone. My grandfather joined them at the bus station, and they all traveled to Addis Ababa - a more than 8-hour journey filled with hope...

When they finally arrived at my uncle Gebeyehou's house, they found out the awful truth. My uncle was dead. It was 1977, and the official story according to sources, was that he had killed himself. How could this be? It couldn't be! Why would he do that?

My uncle was an educated, talented, and intelligent Oromo man who refused to join the government's corruption. He oversaw the Ministry of Planning as an economics expert. He refused to write false statements claiming the economy had improved under the Derg regime. And for that, he paid the ultimate price.

Grief hit my family like a storm. My grandmother lost her only son, the one she had sacrificed so much to raise. My grandmother was forced to get married and forced stay with her husband. But she chose to raise her son as a wise gentleman. Alas! His life was cut short. Grief seems a very small word for an eight-year-old kid seeing her grandma going through such trauma. My mom, already grieving from her divorce, now had to bear the loss of her precious brother. The evidence didn't add up, leaving us with endless questions. Why did this happen? How? What if?

I grew up listening to my grandmother's mourning for her only son, Gebeyehou Firrissa. Her grief echoed throughout our home. No one should be killed for speaking the truth or standing up for what they believe in.

Grandma, Cawwaaqee, grieving in her black outfit

Uncle Gebeyehou whose life was cut short

DURETI (MIMI) TADESSE

Grandpa Firrissa

This kind of tragedy still happens, however, it is now exposed by the media, creating awareness and more resistance. The media coverage helps to bring some closure to families and friends. But for us, the pain and horror of that time still lives on and feels very real.

As if ethnic discrimination wasn't enough, we also faced religious persecution. Following the 1974 communist takeover, Christianity was banned, forcing us to practice our faith in secret. Oromo Christians faced double jeopardy: oppressed as a nation and persecuted as Christians. My mom took an enormous risk and turned our home into an underground church for over 17 years. Growing up I learned to be careful not to be caught by the government while meeting with other Christians. We couldn't sing or preach loudly. Everything had to be done in secret.

It was scary but also kind of exciting. Nighttime was when it got incredibly scary. People would come knocking, demanding to come in. Can you imagine that? Being woken up by loud knocks in the middle of the night? How did we keep our faith alive in such conditions?

My grandma was very tough. She would yell back, asking who was there, and if they didn't answer, she'd start calling for help from the neighbors. You know those moments, right around midnight, when it feels like time could just stop?

Gender discrimination was yet another battle. In a society where male chauvinism is rampant, gender discrimination is seen as normal. The oppression of Oromo women has deep historical roots, with many women taking on the full responsibility of caring for families and managing property in the face of relentless persecution.

I personally escaped rape attempts more than three times. The fear and trauma from those incidents still linger. I lived with multiple fears. There was the fear of the government, fear of being raped, and the fear of being beaten by a bully because my father was not around. Often it was fear after fear, after fear. Why should any woman have to live with such fear or violence?

Being an Oromo woman brings another layer of persecution. Since the late 1880s, Oromo women have shouldered the heavy burden of the struggle against oppression. Many Oromo men involved in the fight for freedom were killed, imprisoned, or fled the country. Other men were forced to go to war by the government. The burden of taking care of both family and property fell on the shoulders of Oromo women. Many mothers were also taken to prisons, leaving their children abandoned. I am a product of the harsh realities Oromo women faced.

Even with these deadliest days at home, it was like stepping into a different world. Mom and Grandma, our superheroes at that time, turned our little house into a fortress of warmth and love. Outside? A whole different story. Every step out the door was a mini adventure in dodging shadows and whispering dangers. Going to school felt like tiptoeing through a minefield, not knowing when things might just blow up.

Every day, every moment was filled with uncertainties. Each knock on the door was an alarm. An alarm warning of someone coming to attack us or alert us to the news of what was going on. It's just a human being. It's just door-to-door. There was no civilized way of communicating. There were no phones, no internet, nothing.

But now, here in the United States, where I seemingly have it all: a phone and an internet connection - I still find myself holding my breath. I often anxiously wait for calls to hear that everyone back home in Oromia are safe. It's those calls that bind us together.

How do I explain that kind of fear? Even though we are oceans apart the thoughts keep haunting me. I need to know they are fine. "Are they okay?" My voice is barely a whisper, more to myself than anyone else.

You see, with every call, it's like I'm trying to build a bridge from here to Oromia with nothing but hope and phone lines. And it's tough, believe me. Two of my siblings, my daughter, nieces, aunts, uncles, and extended family are still back home. They are always with me. They never leave my mind.

Why is it so hard to just get them here? I always wondered!

"Hey, are you safe? What's happening now?" I ask the same questions almost every time. The answers are never enough to soothe the worry that knots up in my gut.

There are moments of calm between the waves of political chaos. Times when people feel connected, when the neighborhood comes together, and things seem almost normal. Then the tension returns, and the calm is gone. If only they could be here with us during those rare, peaceful times. The thought loops around my mind like a mantra. Safer. They'd be safer here in the US, away from all the chaos that keeps everyone on edge. *It's just too much sometimes.*

So, when I tell you about the fear and concerns, it's not just about what might happen. It's about feeling helpless, miles away, trying to hold onto my family with nothing more than phone calls and prayers. It's a thin thread to hang onto, but we hang on because that's what families do. Right?

Sometimes, I find myself thinking back to those early days when fear first crept into my life. I was just a kid, not really understanding what was happening but feeling the immense weight of it all.

Do you know the feeling of waiting? The feeling of uncertainty? As Khaled Hosseini, a U.S. Goodwill Envoy to the UNHCR, the UN Refugee Agency, and the founder of The Khaled Hosseini Foundation, a nonprofit that provides humanitarian assistance to the people of Afghanistan, says, "*Of all the hardships a person had to face, none was more punishing than the simple act of waiting.*"

Surely it is!

Every day, when my sister would go to school, my mom and grandma would be worried until she was safely back home. You know that kind of concern, don't you? The air was always thick with tension. It wasn't just any kind of concern; it was the fear of the unknown, the anxiety that comes from living in a place where political movements could turn a normal day into a nightmare. Ah! Those days of terror!

One of the scariest times was when my sister was forced to stay with other high school students in school overnight to meet with political leaders. Just imagine ninth-grade students questioned about politics. What do they know about politics? Exactly. Nothing. None of us understood why, but I could see the fear in my mom's and grandma's eyes as they left the house to stand with other parents outside the school. Waiting all night. Not knowing what was happening inside the school. I didn't understand politics as a kid, but I could feel the fear and the chaos.

So, my dear readers, can you relate to my story to Phoenix's now? Life was continuously burning us down into ashes, but we were holding on tight!

The flames didn't end there, no they continued to flare up in different forms. Growing up, I faced fear and harassment in so many ways.

RESILIENCE

One of the most terrifying situations in my life was when a group of strange men came to our house, banging on the door and shouting, "Open the door! Open the door!" Their voices were loud and terrifying, echoing through the house throughout the night. Can you imagine the panic that gripped us? As a kid, I would spend my whole night wondering, "Why is this happening to us? Why can't we just be safe in our own homes? Why is being related to a specific ethnicity so arduous?" I wish no child ever had to go through this!

As I reflect on these experiences, I realize that those experiences were the fires that tested and refined me, just like the mythical Phoenix. They burned away the fear and uncertainty, leaving behind a stronger and more resilient version of myself. Just as the Phoenix rises from the ashes, I, too, Dureti "Mimi" Tadesse, have risen from these challenges. I am ready to face whatever comes my way. The story of my life is one of transformation and renewal, and it's a story I hope to share with the world to inspire others who might be going through similar struggles.

These memories of persecution, loss, and resilience have deeply shaped who I am today. They have taught me to appreciate the freedom I have now and to never take it for granted. They have also made me more empathetic towards others who face discrimination and injustice. My experiences have fueled my passion for advocating for human rights and justice. They have also strengthened my faith, reminding me of the power of hope and resilience.

As I look back, I am grateful for the lessons I have learned and the strength I have gained. My journey has been challenging, but it has also been incredibly rewarding. I am proud of the person I have become and the resilience I have developed. My story is a testament to the power of faith, hope, and perseverance. It's a story that I hope will inspire others to rise above their challenges and pursue their dreams, just like the Phoenix rises from the ashes.

So, this is my story, dear reader. A story of trials and triumphs, of ashes and rising. Just like the Phoenix, I have faced my fires and risen anew each time. This is not the end; it's just the beginning of a new chapter in my life.

And you, dear reader, what will your story be? Will you let the fires consume you, or will you rise from the ashes like the Phoenix, stronger and more beautiful than before?

RESILIENCE

Chapter 2
The Nature of Persecution

Section I: Personal Trials

As the sun began to set, casting long shadows across the desolate land, the silence was almost palpable, broken only by the faint rustle of leaves. In these quiet moments, the weight of our situation pressed heavily on us, and fear felt like a tangible presence.

Growing up in Oromia, Ethiopia, my childhood was marred by relentless harassment and fear. Haunting memories that still linger in my mind are of nights when strange men would come to our door, pounding and shouting, "Open the door! Open the door!" Their voices were loud and commanding, filling our home with dread. My grandmother and mother woke up instantly, their concern for us children clear in their faces. Grandma would bravely call out, trying to find out who was outside, while I, along with my siblings, would scramble to find a hiding place. My favorite hiding spot was under my grandmother's dress, standing as close to her as I could, desperately wanting to help but unsure how.

There was no one to call for help—no 911, emergency services, or even a phone in the house. We were completely on our own. The

RESILIENCE

men outside would persist, trying to force their way in. In a desperate attempt to scare them off, Grandma would shout for the neighbors, making a loud "Uuuu Uuuuu Uuuuu" sound, which was a traditional call for help. Luckily, the intruders, not wanting to be seen by the neighbors, would eventually leave. The neighbors would come over, and we would share stories of similar experiences, the fear still fresh in everyone's minds.

Years of this harassment left deep scars on our hearts. Families like ours, without a male figure to stand as a protector, were easy targets. The nights were long, filled with a dread that never seemed to lift, even with the break of dawn. One particular night stands out more vividly than the rest, like a nightmare that refuses to fade. It was raining heavily, the kind of rain that soaked through to your bones. My mother and older siblings were not at home. They had gone to be closer to the hospital because my younger brother was suffering from asthma. My grandmother and I were alone at home. Despite the rain, she sensed something was wrong. She had a strong intuition and could even smell the faint odor of cigarette smoke outside the door.

Suddenly, there was a loud kick on the door, and the intruder tried to break in. My grandmother, holding a metal stick, fearlessly shouted at him to come in if he dared. She was ready to defend our home. The intruder, realizing she was prepared to fight back, fled into the night. We could hear his footsteps fading away. That night, we stayed awake until dawn, the terror of what could have been keeping sleep at bay. The next morning, Grandma reported the incident to the community elders and the police. Mom heard about the situation and hired a repairman to help repair the door. The church team, bless them, were always there for us. They took turns spending the night, keeping watch to make sure we were safe. The men from the church were like silent guardians, protecting us for years and giving us the courage to face another day.

Despite their help, the fear of persecution never left us. Growing up in Oromia, Ethiopia, I was surrounded by uncertainty and danger. The shift from monarchy to socialism brought new challenges, especially for us Christian Oromo. We were viewed with suspicion, and our language and faith were seen as threats. The government's harsh policies were meant to break our spirits and silence our voices.

I remember sitting together at night, tense and quiet, listening to soldiers patrolling outside. Their footsteps echoed in the darkness, a constant reminder they could come for us at any moment. Despite this, I refused to let fear control me. I wanted to rise above the persecution, to prove we were more than just victims.

But not all dangers came under the cover of night. One day, under the sun's bright light, two government workers' family members came to our house and called me out, asking how I was, luring me with their false kindness. They seemed friendly, and I, unaware of the trap they were setting, followed them toward a familiar neighborhood. Next to the high school nearby, they said, "Let us stop by and say hello to a friend." It was a house I recognized. Once inside, they led me into an unfamiliar room. Before I could react, they left the room, and I was trapped inside with a drunk man I had never seen before.

Panic set in as I realized I was trapped. The man blocked the door, and there was no way out except through a window. Without thinking, I jumped out, not knowing how far the drop was. I hit the ground hard, but I forced myself up and I ran. I ran as fast as I could, afraid that the man might be chasing me. When I finally reached home, I slowed down, trying to steady my breathing and calm my racing heart. I was afraid of how my mother would react if she found out what happened. In our culture, girls were often blamed if anything happened to them, and I didn't want to bring shame to my family, nor did I want to face punishment.

Years later, I came to realize the gravity of what had happened that day. I had narrowly escaped becoming a victim of trafficking, a fate that would have changed my life forever. It took me years to fully comprehend it. It wasn't until I was older and involved in anti-trafficking work that I saw how close I had come to being a victim. A fellow volunteer once told me, "You're a hero, you're brave, you saved yourself." Her words finally made me see that I *had* been brave that day, even though I hadn't acknowledged it for many years.

As a child, I wanted to make my mother and grandmother proud. I didn't want them to be seen as just other women raising a child in tough times. My mother and grandmother were heroes, and I wanted to be a daughter who could honor them. I worked hard in school, sharing what little I had with my classmates. I would break my pencil in half, keeping the part with the eraser for myself and giving the other half to a friend. It was a small gesture, but it made me feel like I was making a difference, no matter how modest.

Throughout these harrowing experiences, I often felt anger towards my father. He had a good income and owned a pharmacy and properties, yet he wasn't there to provide for us or protect us. My beloved siblings and I wished he had been with us, even if it meant less money. His absence made us vulnerable to danger, and I blamed him for not being there when we needed him most.

With my siblings in 2006 (left to right) - Me, Million, Eyob, Serawit, Lideya and Temesgen.

In time, I forgave my father, though it wasn't easy. I reconnected with him before he passed away and tried to support him as best as I could. But the anger lingered, fueled by the fear and helplessness I felt as a child. I longed for a father figure, someone who could have kept us safe and spared us from the many horrors we faced.

These experiences have left a deep impact on me. Even today, I struggle with the trauma of those years. I feel a constant need to be home before dark, as if the night still holds the same dangers it did when I was a child.

As I grew older, I felt a deep connection to the people of the countryside, even though I grew up in the city. I loved spending time with them, listening to their stories, and sharing in their struggles. They had so little, but their spirit and resilience gave me hope. The women in Ethiopia, Oromia, were not just oppressed; they were invisible, their voices silenced by a system that treated them as less than human. Many girls I went to school with became pregnant outside of marriage, often feeling pressured to consider abortion due to the stigma or lack of resources to raise a child. I also know the harrowing reality of women being raped while gathering firewood or fetching water from creeks—something I observed firsthand during visits to my grandmother's coffee farm in the countryside. I remember seeing girls running in fear when they sensed danger on their way to get water. Tragically, some of them died of HIV before they had the chance to truly live. These injustices fueled my desire to make a difference and to give back to the community that had shaped me.

I couldn't just enjoy the comforts of my life in America while my people were suffering. The contrast between my life here and the life I left behind was too stark to ignore. How could I find peace knowing young girls and women were being raped? That women were away from homes and children gathering firewood to sell. They were walking miles and miles, facing horrific violence just to make 25 cents a day on average for a living? How could I enjoy my freedom when so many were still trapped in the same cycle of oppression that I had escaped?

This woman gathered firewood and walking miles to sell it in the city

These questions drove me to start a non-profit organization, a way to fight for the rights of those who had been forgotten. It wasn't easy, and there were times when I doubted myself, but I knew I couldn't turn my back on my people. I couldn't just stand by and watch history continue to repeated itself.

RESILIENCE

Looking back, I see that my goals have always been about helping others, no matter how big or small the impact. My personal goals may have changed, but the core of who I am remains the same. I still want to be that little girl who broke her pencil into two pieces and shared it with her friend. The same little girl who cares enough to make a difference.

There are days when the memories of those I've lost and the hardships I've faced threaten to overwhelm me. But then I think of my mother, my grandmother and other family members, and the church team who stood by us when no one else would, of the people who have believed in me, and I realize I cannot give up.

Persecution tries to break you, to make you feel small and powerless. But it can also ignite a fire within you, pushing you to rise above it, to fight back. It can turn suffering into strength and victims into warriors. I've learned to manage my fear and anxiety, but they never completely go away. The trauma is a part of me, shaping my actions and decisions.

Despite all this, I have come a long way. I've learned to communicate my experiences, to share my story, and to understand the emotions that come with it. I know that I am stronger now, but the shadows of fear still linger, a reminder of a childhood marked by danger and the struggle to survive.

Section II: Broader Context

1974 marks one of the darkest chapters in Ethiopia's long and storied history. The winds of change swept through the country with a ferocity that few could have predicted. The seemingly unshakable Emperor Haile Selassie, who had ruled Ethiopia for forty-four years, was suddenly dethroned in a military coup. The Derg, a group of military officers, seized power, ushering in a period of unprecedented turmoil and bloodshed. The Ethiopia I knew as a child, with its rich cultural heritage and deep-seated traditions, was rapidly disintegrating into chaos and fear.

In Nekemte city, where I spent my early years, the news of the emperor's downfall was met with disbelief and dread. We did not have televisions or newspapers to keep us informed, but the radio—our lifeline to the outside world—brought us the chilling updates. The voices on the airwaves spoke of a new regime, one that promised equality and justice but delivered terror and oppression. As the stories filtered through our small town, the atmosphere became charged with anxiety. The older generation, who had lived through the emperor's reign, sensed this was the beginning of something far more sinister.

The Derg's rise to power marked a significant shift in Ethiopia's political and social landscape. In their bid to consolidate power, the military junta turned to the Soviet Union for support. This alliance introduced Ethiopia to the brutal tactics of Marxist-Leninist regimes. There was state-sponsored violence, forced collectivization, and the suppression of all forms of dissent. The old ways of life, steeped in centuries of tradition, were being systematically dismantled. The very air seemed thick with fear as if the land itself was mourning the loss of its identity.

One of the most significant events of this period was the Edget Bhibret Zamacha campaign, launched by the Derg as part of its efforts to reshape Ethiopian society. Under the guise of national development, tens of thousands of students and teachers were forcibly relocated from cities to rural areas. This campaign was presented as a way to bridge the gap between urban and rural communities, but in reality, it was a thinly veiled attempt to neutralize potential opposition to the regime.

As a young girl, I remember the excitement and confusion that accompanied the arrival of buses filled with these student volunteers. We were made to line the roads, singing songs of welcome, unaware of the grim reality behind the smiles of those students. To us children, it was an event, something different in our otherwise routine lives. But to the students, it was the beginning of a nightmare. The students, 11th grade though university students, along with their teachers, were being sent away from their families, from the safety of their homes, to live and work in unfamiliar and often hostile environments.

The government claimed this was a develop initiative to improve the lives of the rural poor. But the whispers that reached us told a different story. Some said that the government was dispersing students to prevent them from organizing against the regime. Others believed that the Derg were simply trying to entrench its power by indoctrinating the youth. The truth was far darker. These so-called volunteer programs forced the youth to work on government farms. For many, especially the young girls, these fields became places of horror. The lack of supervision led to widespread abuse and sexual violence. Countless girls returned home pregnant; their lives forever altered. Desperate and ashamed, many attempted to abort their pregnancies using poisons that often led to their deaths. The fields, intended to foster growth, became graveyards for dreams and lives alike.

The Derg's paranoia knew no bounds. The government's reach extended into every home and every relationship. The government frequently used children as cheerleaders for their revolutionary agenda, training them to chant slogans like 'Future Generation Militia' and involving them in events organized by government officials. During the 17 years of Derg rule, no one seemed to care about children missing school. In fact, families could be accused of wrongdoing if they allowed their children to attend school instead of participating in these government-selected events.

RESILIENCE

> I was pulled out of elementary school
> to participate in a program called
> 'Future Generation Militia' (Tadagi Militia),
> causing me to miss many of my regular classes.

Children, once obedient and respectful, were now brainwashed by the state. They returned from their assignments with new ideas, often challenging their parents with the rhetoric they had been taught. Family life started falling apart as political beliefs split households. Brothers turned against brothers, fathers against sons, as the government's influence seeped into the most sacred of bonds.

With the Derg firmly in control, Ethiopia entered a period of extreme repression. The government introduced a series of draconian laws aimed at crushing any form of dissent. Curfews were imposed, and anyone found outside after dark risked being shot on sight. Random arrests and summary executions became terrifyingly common, and the streets of Addis Ababa were often littered with the bodies of those who had been accused of opposing the regime.

The reach of the Derg was long, although we were far from the capital we lived in constant fear in our small town in Nekemte. The radio was our primary source of news, but it was also a tool of propaganda. We heard many stories of families being torn apart. Ther were reports of people disappearing in the middle of the night, never to be seen again. My grandmother and my mom, women of incredible strength and faith, would listen intently to the news. Their faces set in a mask of worry. They knew that we were not immune to the violence spreading across the country.

The Derg's paranoia was all-encompassing. Anyone could be a target—students, teachers, farmers, even government workers. It didn't matter if you were guilty or innocent; what mattered was if you were perceived as a threat. The government didn't have the time or the inclination to investigate accusations. If you were suspected of being involved with an opposition group, you were as good as dead.

One particularly harrowing memory stands out from this time. Our neighbor, a kind gentleman, was accused of being a member of a political group opposed to the Derg. One day, he was simply gone. We later learned that he had been executed in the street, his body left as a warning to others. His family, like so many others, was shattered by the loss. They had done nothing wrong, but in the eyes of the government, they were guilty by association.

The violence reached its peak during what became known as the Red Terror. This was a period of intense repression, where the Derg sought to eliminate all opposition through a campaign of terror. Once bustling with life, the streets of Addis Ababa (Finfinnee) were transformed into a battleground. Families lived in constant fear that their loved ones would be taken away, never to return. The Red Terror was not just a political purge; it was a genocide against those who dared to dream of a different Ethiopia.

In the countryside, many were taken to Addis Ababa's Ma'ekelawi Prison and Addis Ababa's Karchale Prison. Many others were held in Nekemte Karchale Prison. The wives and children of political prisoners suffered greatly. We were somewhat insulated from the worst of the violence and did not see dead bodies in the streets. However, the radio broadcasts were filled with stories of mass executions of bodies left in the streets as gruesome warnings to others. My grandmother and mother would gather us together, their voices trembling as they prayed for the safety of our family and for the souls of those lost. My mother, a prayer warrior, would plan overnight prayer sessions, praying through the long, terrifying nights. It was a time of great fear, made all the worse by the uncertainty of it all. There were no rules, no laws that could protect us. The government had absolute power, and it wielded it with deadly efficiency.

I remember one evening, the sun setting in a blaze of red across the horizon when the fear became almost too much to bear. We had heard rumors that the government was planning a sweep through our area, rounding up anyone suspected of disloyalty. My mother, usually so calm and composed, was visibly shaken. She instructed us to stay inside, to keep the lights off, and to remain silent no matter what we heard outside. That night, I barely slept, the sounds of distant gunfire echoing in my ears, wondering if the soldiers would come for us next. Later, I found out that the gunfire was from a man, who was a father of 4 children, who killed himself before the government army could arrest him.

In 1977, as if the internal strife wasn't enough, Ethiopia found itself embroiled in a brutal conflict with Somalia over the Ogden region. This war was devastating, not just for those who fought in it but for the entire nation. The Derg, desperate to maintain its hold on power, began forcibly conscripting young boys and men to fight on the front lines. These boys, many of them just teenagers, were ripped from their families and sent to die in a conflict they barely understood.

I remember the day when the soldiers came to our town, rounding up boys as young as fourteen and fifteen. The government didn't care whether they were ready to fight or not; they were just bodies to be thrown into the grinder of war. I watched in horror as boys from my neighborhood were loaded onto trucks, their faces pale with fear. They tried to put on brave faces, singing songs of victory as they were driven away, but we all knew that most of them would never return.

My grandmother was a woman of deep faith, and every time we

heard the trucks passing by, she would whisper a prayer for the boys. "God be with them," she would say, her voice filled with sorrow. "Who knows if they'll come back?" And they didn't. The boys who were taken that day, like so many others before and after them, very few returned. Their families were left to mourn, with no bodies to bury, no graves to visit, just the lingering pain of loss. One of them was a young man named Adugna Mekonin, an orphaned teenager who had lived with my parents for many years. He was shot during the war and returned home disabled, forever changed by the conflict.

The war with Eritrea (called Key Kokeb - it means Red Star) was just one of many conflicts that tore Ethiopia apart during this period. The ongoing civil war with Eritrea, the Red Star, and the relentless purges of the Derg all contributed to a sense of hopelessness that pervaded every aspect of life. It was as if the entire country was at war with itself, and there was no end in sight.

As if war and political repression weren't enough, Ethiopia was also struck by a severe drought that ravaged the northern regions between 1972 and 1975. The drought and famine, which primarily affected Wollo and Tigray, killed thousands of people and displaced countless more. Those who survived the famine were forced to flee their homes, seeking refuge wherever they could find it.

In our town, we witnessed the arrival of buses filled with famine survivors, people who had been driven to the brink of death by hunger. I will never forget the sight of those skeletal figures stepping off the buses, their clothes hanging off their emaciated bodies, their eyes hollow with despair. The mothers clutched their babies to their chests, the children too weak to cry, too malnourished to move.

The community did what it could to help, but we had little to offer. The people of Wollaga generously offered land for the displaced to settle and gathered donations, including food and basic necessities. However, it was never enough. The image of a mother cleaning her baby with leaves, the child too weak to even sit up, is burned into my memory. My grandmother warned us to stay back, fearing that we might catch diseases from the desperate, starving people who had been packed into those buses like cattle.

The drought was a tragedy within a tragedy, a crisis within a crisis. The world responded with aid, and songs like 'We Are the World' raised awareness and funds for charities like USA for Africa. But for those of us who witnessed it firsthand, the drought was a reminder of how fragile life is and how quickly it can be taken away.

Throughout all of this, our faith was the only thing that kept us going. But even that was under attack. The Derg, in its quest to control every aspect of life, turned its attention to religion. Churches were closed, Christian worship was outlawed, and those who continued to practice their faith were persecuted mercilessly. Our home became a refuge for those who sought to worship in secret. Apart from our home being available for the homeless due to their Christian beliefs, our home was also open for students who walked long distances from the countryside to school. My mother took responsibility for coordinating weddings and helping the underground church and young adults who didn't have family members nearby. Many got married in our home, and I enjoyed being the candleholder or flower girl.

I was just a child, and while I was enjoying being the flower girl, I also remember the fear that came with carrying meals to prisoners and dropping off food at the local jail's gates under the guards' watchful eyes. For me, it was simply something my mother asked me to do, but in reality, it was an act of defiance—an act that could have cost us our lives. The government was always watching, always listening, and any sign of disobedience was met with swift and brutal punishment.

My grandmother never hesitated to speak her mind, even to the government officials who tried to intimidate us. She was fearless, a trait I admired but didn't fully understand until much later. My mother, on the other hand, was quieter, more reserved, but her resolve was just as strong. From these two women, I learned the power of resilience—the ability to endure, survive, and keep faith even in the darkest of times.

The experiences of my childhood, shaped by war, starvation, and persecution, have left an indelible mark on me. They taught me that survival is not just about physical endurance but also about maintaining the strength of the spirit. In comparing my experiences with other instances of persecution, such as the Russian Bolshevik Revolution of 1917 or the Albanian Revolution, I see the same patterns of oppression, violence, and the silencing of dissent. But I also see the same resilience—the same will to survive and to fight for what is right.

The Ethiopian people, much like those in Rwanda during the

1990s or the oppressed under Hitler's regime in Germany, faced unimaginable horrors. Yet, the human spirit, with its remarkable adaptability, continues to find ways to persevere. It is in our nature to fight for survival, to seek out light in the darkness, and to rise again, much like the Phoenix from its ashes.

My story, though deeply personal, also reflects the broader human experience. It is a testament to the strength that lies within us all—the strength to endure, resist, and overcome. In sharing this story, I hope to remind those who live in more stable and peaceful parts of the world of the fragility of freedom and the importance of vigilance in protecting it.

RESILIENCE

Chapter 3
Personal Transformation and the Trials of Persecution

Section I: Facing Adversity – The Dawale Arrest and Torture

I reflected on the meaning of resilience, not just as a concept but as a lived experience. I had come to understand that resilience was not just about surviving adversity but about transforming through it. In every challenge I faced, I learned that purpose was forged in pain. This realization came to the forefront of my mind as my journey took me through trials of internal struggles, as well as the brutal reality of external oppression.

My journey of personal transformation began in Finfinnee (Addis Ababa) city, where I met my husband, Danny (Daniel Daffa), while I was attending music school.

RESILIENCE

Me and my husband, Danny

He was a student at Addis Ababa University, resuming his education after spending a decade in Ma'ekelawi political prison. His time in prison left deep emotional and physical scars, and even after his release, his life was constantly under threat. In those days, the tension in Finfinnee (Addis Ababa) was palpable. Political movements driven by university students were frequently met with harsh government crackdowns. My husband, Danny, being a political prisoner, was constantly watched the government secret service. It seemed like there was no escape from their prying eyes. They followed him to restaurants, on the streets, and even when we tried to have a quiet moment, they were always there, watching.

One incident stands out in my memory. We were having a meal

at a restaurant near 4 Kilo when Danny noticed a secret service agent sitting near us, trying to eavesdrop on our conversation. Sensing danger, we decided to quietly slip away. To avoid being followed, we pretended to go to the restroom. We watched from behind a wall as the agent, thinking we had left, ran out in a hurry. We were relieved but knew we couldn't keep living like this, under constant surveillance and threat.

Our life in Finfinee (Addis Ababa) was becoming more unsafe. Addis Ababa University students kept on boycotting and chanting slogans against the government that we could hear all night long. We also worried for family members and friends who were in the University compound because we heard gunshots.

Danny, traumatized by his time in prison, was determined to leave the country. His mistrust extended even to family members, a sign of the deep scars left by his years of incarceration. When he received a scholarship from Emporia Kansas University in the U.S., it felt like a miracle—a chance for a new beginning away from the constant threat of persecution.

The day he was supposed to leave, his family, friends, and I went to the airport to bid him farewell. For many of us, it was such a relief when Danny was finally set to leave, but his brother, Girma Daffa, who never trusted the government, decided to wait at the airport until the plane actually took off. Close to midnight, just before departure, a couple of government secret service agents boarded the plane, confiscated Danny's passport, and forcibly removed him in handcuffs. From the Parking Lot near the lobby, Girma caught sight of the agents taking him away and immediately ran after them, shouting, 'Where are you taking my brother? Where are you taking my brother?'

After Danny was taken into the Secret Service car, the agents contacted their superiors by radio and mentioned that they had been seen by Danny's brother. Following instructions, they were ordered to drop Danny off at the Gion Hotel. Danny's brother, who had followed the car the entire way, was able to retrieve him from the hotel.

This ongoing harassment and the fact that Danny was forcibly removed from the plane convinced him that he had no choice but to flee the country. He also made it clear to me that if he left without me, I would be in danger as well, given my association with him.

The next chapter of my life would be marked by a series of brutal encounters with the government—moments that tested not only my physical endurance but the very core of my identity and beliefs. I would soon find myself at the mercy of forces I had never imagined encountering, forces that would strip me of my freedom and challenge every ounce of resilience I had built.

And yet, in those moments, resilience was all I had left. My faith, my inner strength, and my hope for a better future became my only shield against the onslaught of brutality. What followed were some of the darkest days of my life—arrests, torture, and the terrifying uncertainty of not knowing if I would ever see my loved ones again.

The journey to freedom is never easy, especially when the path is marked by fear, uncertainty, and unimaginable suffering. As Danny, Kebebew, Mohamed (one of the guides who joined us on our way to help cross the border) and I traveled towards the border to flee the country together, a mix of hope and dread filled the air. Every checkpoint we passed, every time the bus or train stopped, my heart raced. The soldiers, with their stern faces and unforgiving gazes, boarded the buses and trains, inspecting everyone, and I could feel their eyes lingering on me longer than necessary. Were we being followed? Did they know we were trying to flee the country?

At that moment, panic gripped me. My thoughts spiraled—*What am I going to say? What will happen if they search me? Will they find my identification documents, my school transcripts, or my ID card? Will they arrest us?* The questions came rushing into my mind, leaving me in a state of sheer terror. I tried to rehearse answers to stay calm, but the fear of being discovered overwhelmed me.

It was a long journey and we had to stop and spend the night before continuing towards the border. That night, I was already uncomfortable when I noticed the nervousness of one of the guides. I prayed desperately. *God, is this the right thing to do? Will we make it?* The Holy Spirit whispered a warning to me—I felt deep in my heart that we would not succeed in crossing the border. But how could I turn back? My husband, Danny, was with me with his two friends, and if something were to happen to them, I knew I would carry that regret for the rest of my life. I couldn't stop. Despite the growing sense of doom that hung over us like a shadow, I had to keep moving.

RESILIENCE

As we neared the border, I tried my best to blend in. I dressed like the locals—Somalians and Oromo Hararghe—hoping my disguise would protect me. The market was bustling with activity, and for a brief moment, I thought we might slip through unnoticed. But the atmosphere was tense, and there was talk of government soldiers being killed by contraband business people near the Ethiopia-Djibouti border in the area just two weeks before our arrival. Fear gripped the marketplace, and before I knew it, the military junta was upon us. They arrested me, my husband Danny, and two of his friends, Kebebew and Mohamed. The overwhelming terror that followed is hard to describe. They did not know we were together until they found my picture in one of the wallets.

They took my husband away first, separating us. We weren't allowed to speak to each other. The unknown gnawed at me—*What were they doing to him? Would they kill him? Where were they taking us?* They kept us apart to ensure we couldn't communicate. Every moment felt like an eternity, filled with uncertainty and fear of what might happen next.

That day, they took us to a local prison near the train station at Ethiopia-Djibouti border. It was a small, crude facility where prisoners were held while traveling to or from Djibouti. The conditions were horrific. My husband and his friends were locked in small separate rooms used as restrooms filled with human waste. The stench was unbearable, and I couldn't imagine the torment they must have felt, confined in such filth. I was forced to sleep outside, exposed to the sweltering desert heat during the day and the terrifying darkness of the night. There was no food, no water, and no place to relieve myself except the open field, all while soldiers stood watch, leering and pointing their guns at me. I felt utterly dehumanized.

During one of those terrifying nights, a soldier attempted to rape me. The fear was so intense that words alone cannot describe it. I prayed—*Jesus, please save me!* And in that moment of despair, a train horn sounded in the distance. The sound grew louder and louder, and as the train approached, a group of prisoners disembarked and were brought to the prison. I've never felt so relieved to see more prisoners arriving. They crowded around me, speaking in different languages, but it didn't matter. The presence of others saved me that night. The soldier who had intended to harm me could no longer act with impunity. My prayers had been answered, and I was spared from the unimaginable.

The days in Dawale prison blurred together in a haze of thirst, hunger, and pain. The weather was scorching,—over 100 degrees, with no shelter from the sun. At night, we would huddle together, struggling to find a space on the hard, uneven ground. One boy, only about 13 or 14 years old, noticed me struggling to find a place to sleep. Despite his own suffering, he flattened a cardboard box and offered it to me as a mat. In the midst of such a terrifying an dark place, his act of kindness shone like a beacon. But even that moment of ease was short-lived, as the rain began to fall it forced us to crowd together under the small metal cover of the prison to avoid getting soaked.

RESILIENCE

For three days, I hadn't eaten, and my body felt like it was slowly shutting down. A kind man who had given me 20 Ethiopian Birr earlier appeared once more like a guardian angel. I found a way to let my husband know I had 20 Birr. Even 20 Birr was a blessing since the military junta took the money we had on hand. Danny somehow found a way to speak to the guards and buy a small bag of pasta. Relief washed over me for a brief moment, but it quickly turned into chaos as we were all so desperate, so hungry. People (prisoners) fought for that small plastic bag of food, driven by pure survival. I only managed two bites before it was torn from my hands, and that was all I had to sustain me. For days, those two bites were all that stood between me and complete collapse, as I felt myself growing weaker by the hour, clinging to hope.

Most of the soldiers showed no mercy. One of them even robbed my husband, stealing the ring from his finger while he was locked in the filth of his prison room. The humiliation was unbearable.

The torture soon followed. They beat me relentlessly, demanding that I confess we were fleeing the country. At first, I felt the shock of every blow, but as the beatings continued, my body went numb. The agony was unbearable, but I refused to break. Again, I prayed— *Jesus please save me.*

They took Danny away again, and I didn't see him for an entire day. The fear they had done something to him consumed me. When they finally brought him back, I was overwhelmed with relief, though the terror of what could have happened still lingered.

Despite everything, Danny and I tried to use every opportunity to communicate. He coached me on what to say during interrogations. He was convinced they would kill him, but he was determined to protect me and his friends. Prayers, his strength, and his friend's strength gave me the courage to keep going, even when everything seemed hopeless.

After three days in Dawale, we were transferred to Dire Dawa prison, handcuffed together—my left hand shackled to Danny's right, and Kebebew and Mohamed, also handcuffed together. The train journey to Dire Dawa was torturous, both physically and mentally. We were crammed into a container meant for transporting straw for animals, with nothing to hold onto as the train swayed. The discomfort was immense, but the opportunity to communicate with my husband, even for a brief moment, was a small blessing. In those moments we communicated how we could save one another!

In Dire Dawa, the conditions were just as horrific, if not worse. The prison was overcrowded, filthy, and reeked of human waste. The women's cell was a particular nightmare, with overflowing restrooms and flies swarming everywhere. At night, the police would come to our cell, shining flashlights and trying to exploit the women. We were terrified every time we saw the beam of a flashlight approaching, knowing what their intentions were. We couldn't sleep, always on high alert, fearing for our lives and dignity.

After two weeks in Dire Dawa prison, they moved us once again, this time to Ma'ekelawi, an infamous political prison in Addis Ababa (Finfinnee). The journey was long and grueling, and we were forced to spend a night in Adama City's local prison, where I was placed in a prison cell that flooded during the night. I had to stand on a metal bed frame and hold onto the roof to avoid being swept away by the floodwaters. The constant fear of drowning, combined with exhaustion and hunger, pushed me to the edge of my endurance.

When we finally arrived at Ma'ekelawi, it felt like stepping into the gates of hell.

Having already spent over a decade in this prison, Danny seemed almost at ease, reconnecting with old friends and comrades as if stepping back into a world he had never truly left. But for those around him, his return was heartbreaking. Danny's comrades were devastated to see him back, especially with me at his side. They didn't believe I would withstand the brutal torture, and they feared I might not be able to protect them. In situations like this, it often takes just one person breaking for others to fall—if I admitted to fleeing the country, it could have put every Oromo political prisoner, many of whom had already endured over a decade behind bars, in grave danger.

I never knew if the torture would break me, and I admit, it was a constant, looming threat—not just to my life but to countless others. Years later, comrades Mulugeta Mosisa and Nagari Fayisa shared with me how terrifying the situation had been for all Oromo political prisoners during that time. The fear was palpable, not just for themselves but for the entire movement. But Mohamed and I were resolute. We couldn't allow ourselves to give up, knowing that

Danny's life, along with Kebebew's and so many others, hung in the balance.

With God's help, Mohamed and I found the strength to endure. Through that strength, we were able to protect them— save their lives, and in doing so, preserve the spirit of the Oromo resistance.

As it was my first time in prison, I was utterly terrified. The interrogations began almost immediately. I was beaten repeatedly. They wanted me to confess to crimes I hadn't committed, and when I refused, the beatings intensified. The torture continued; each session was more brutal than the last. One particular time, they took me to an underground building, covered my eyes so that I wouldn't see my surroundings, tied me up, and hung me upside down (see below sample image).

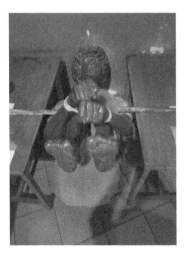

One of the torture styles. This image is taken from the Red Terror Martyrs' Memorial Museum in Finfinnee (Addis Ababa).

RESILIENCE

I screamed and talked in my native language, Afaan Oromo, when they started beating on the bottom of my feet and my lower back. I called Jesus to save me many times. But I was told not to speak my language, and they said let your Jesus come and save you. My body, already weak from days of torture, felt like it was being torn apart. I couldn't breathe, and I lost consciousness. I was not sure for how long I was tortured hanging. When I awoke, I was lying on the floor, unable to move. A guard dragged me out of the torture room and threw me into a dark room, a cell with two mentally unstable women. While the guard dragged me to the cell, I asked myself, nervously confused, what was next and what was happening to Danny and his friends. We passed by a room, a cell with a door slightly cracked open. I saw hands up the sign Do not give up, be strong from Mohamed, who was tortured before I was tortured in the prison basement. The hands-up sign from Mohamed lifted me up amazingly and told me that we all are on the same page resisting.

In the cell where I was thrown, one of the mentally unstable women was pregnant, and I later learned that she had been beaten so badly that the baby inside her was also injured. The other woman was younger but had clearly lost her mind from the torture she had endured. The room was dark, and the air was thick with despair. The two women screamed and cried through the night, their pain echoing through the small space. I prayed constantly, calling out to Jesus to save me. I clung to my faith, even when it seemed like all hope was lost. I knew I had to stay strong, not just for myself but for Danny and his friends. I couldn't afford to break.

The torture had taken its toll on my body. My back was covered in wounds, and every movement sent a wave of pain through me. Danny had warned me not to scream too loudly during the torture sessions because the soldiers didn't want the other prisoners to hear the screams. They would force a ball made out of socks into the mouths of prisoners who screamed too loudly. The ball was filthy, covered in blood and vomit from years of use. The thought of having that put in my mouth terrified me. I did everything I could to keep from screaming, even as the pain became unbearable.

There was one particular interrogator named Afera, brutal and heartless, who worked under Tefera supervision (nickname Wukaw) who seemed to take pleasure in inflicting pain. One day, he entered my cell and ordered me to stand up. I could barely move, but I forced myself to my feet. He told me to lift my foot and showed him the wound, and as I did, he kicked me in the wound. I collapsed, unable to hold myself up any longer. The pregnant woman in the cell screamed, "Leave her alone!" but the interrogator only sneered. He bent down, preparing to kick me again, but a guard intervened, holding him back. I never understood why, but I felt a flicker of relief at that moment. It was brief, but it reminded me that there were small moments of mercy even in the darkest places.

Despite everything, my faith remained my guiding light. Now, when I think about it, I kept repeating a verse from the Bible in my mind: *Father, forgive them, for they know not what they do.* At the time, I didn't understand why I was being subjected to such cruelty, but I held onto the belief that there was a greater purpose behind my suffering.

Section II: Personal Growth and Transformation:

Looking back, it's hard to believe that I survived those months in prison. The physical and emotional scars will stay with me forever, but they have also shaped me into the person I am today. My time in prison taught me the power of resilience and the strength of the human spirit. It had forced me to confront my own mortality and to find a deeper sense of purpose in the face of unimaginable suffering.

My perception of persecution evolved during those months. At first, I saw it as an unbearable injustice—a punishment for being who I was: Oromo, Christian, and a voice for freedom. The government sought to break us, to strip away our identities and our will to fight. But as the days wore on, I began to see persecution differently. It was no longer just a tool of oppression but a test of endurance, a trial that would shape my character and fortify my spirit. It became a crucible in which I discovered strength I never knew I had.

There were moments when I felt broken, unable to withstand any more beatings, sleepless nights, or the uncertainty of whether I would ever see my husband or family and friends again. But those were the moments that defined me. They pushed me to pray harder, to cling to hope more fiercely, and to stand strong not only for myself but for the others imprisoned with me. My faith became my anchor, and I refused to let my spirit be crushed.

DURETI (MIMI) TADESSE

One of the greatest lessons I learned in that dark prison cell was the importance of human connection and the presence of the Holy Spirit. The prisoners— men and women from different backgrounds, different ethnic groups, and different political affiliations—became my family. We supported one another, shared what little food we had, and encouraged each other through every hardship. In that hellish place where we were supposed to feel isolated and alone, we found solidarity. We shared our stories in the women's cell, hopes and prayers. Even the smallest gesture—a thumbs-up, a kind word, or a piece of food—meant everything. It was through these small acts of humanity that I realized the true meaning of resilience

When I finally left the dark room where I had been kept with the mentally unstable women and was transferred to a larger cell with other political prisoners, it felt like I was returning to the light after being lost in darkness. The other women welcomed me as one of their own. They had all been there for years, enduring the same suffering I had just begun to experience. Their strength inspired me, and I drew courage from their stories of survival. Yet, even among these strong women, I saw moments when their hope began to fray. There were nights when some wept silently, withdrawing from the group, haunted by nightmares or the crushing fear that freedom might never come. Sleeplessness plagued many of them; some resorted to taking sleeping pills just to escape the torment, if only for a few hours. In those dark moments, when despair felt too heavy to bear, I turned to prayer, inviting them to join me. Praying together became a beacon of hope in that cold, oppressive space. We became more than just prisoners—we became a community of survivors, bound together by our shared pain and determination to endure.

My husband, Danny, had endured far more suffering than I had. He had spent over a decade in Ma'ekelawi before, and his experience helped guide me through the worst moments. He would find ways to send me notes, hidden in bars of soap or dropped discreetly during meal times. He, his comrades' and his cell-met friends' words of encouragement lifted my spirit, reminding me that I was not alone in my suffering. He had been through this before and had survived, and they believed I would, too. Their unwavering belief in our survival became a source of strength for me, and I clung to it, even in the most hopeless moments.

One of the most profound moments came when I received a Bible smuggled into my meal by another prisoner. It was a simple, small New Testament, but to me, it was a lifeline. I read its pages over and over, finding solace in the words of faith and hope. The Bible became my refuge in that prison, a reminder that, despite everything, God was with me. My faith sustained me through the darkest nights, through the pain of torture, and through the fear of the unknown.

After months of enduring this nightmare, I came to realize that persecution had not broken me. Instead, it had forged in me an unshakable belief in the power of hope and the importance of standing strong in the face of adversity. I learned that my true strength did not lie in my physical body, which had been battered and beaten, but in my spirit, which remained unbroken.

Over time, my perception of persecution continued to evolve. Initially, I viewed it as a purely negative force, something to be feared and avoided at all costs. But as I endured the hardships of imprisonment, I began to see it differently. Persecution, as cruel and unjust as it was, also brought clarity. It forced me to confront who I was, what I stood for, and what I was willing to sacrifice for my beliefs.

In the early days of my imprisonment, I was consumed by fear— fear of the unknown, fear for my husband and fear for my own survival. But as the days turned into weeks and then months, I realized that fear could no longer control me. I had faced the worst of what the government could do to me, and I was still standing. The soldiers, the interrogators, and the torturers had tried to break me, but they failed. I had endured. And in that endurance, I found a new sense of freedom.

Freedom, I realized, was not just the absence of chains or the ability to move about as I pleased. True freedom was the power to maintain my integrity and my faith, even in the face of overwhelming oppression. It was the ability to hold onto my beliefs and my sense of self, no matter how much the world tried to strip them away. The more they tried to dehumanize me, the more I clung to my humanity. The more they tried to silence me, the louder my inner voice became.

RESILIENCE

The world outside the prison walls was not as it had been before. I had changed. I was no longer the same person who had entered those dark cells months earlier. I was stronger, more determined, and more aware of the power of resilience. I understood the value of freedom in a way that I never could have before. Having experienced life without it, I now cherish it more than ever.

My time in prison also deepened my connection to my Oromo identity. In the face of persecution, I began to seek answers about my heritage, my culture, and the history of my people. I started to read more about the Gadaa system, the traditional democratic governance system of the Oromo people, and I gained a deeper appreciation for my ancestors' struggles. This knowledge became a part of my healing process, helping me to reclaim a sense of pride in who I was and where I came from.

The persecution I endured did not destroy me—it transformed me. It gave me a deeper understanding of the human spirit's capacity for resilience and instilled in me a sense of responsibility to share my story with others. Many people who have been through similar experiences struggle to talk about what happened to them, and I understand why. The trauma runs deep, and for some, revisiting those memories is too painful. But I chose to share my story because I believe that we can heal ourselves and others through sharing.

In prison, I witnessed the worst of humanity—brutality, injustice, and cruelty. But I also witnessed the best of humanity. Even in the darkest moments, there were glimmers of hope and compassion. My family and friends came to drop food, money, and other necessary items through the prison window. The prisoners who gave me a thumbs-up, or the comrades who made me feel better, or the girl who smuggled a Bible to me, or the young boy who gave me a cardboard box to sleep on, all demonstrated the power of kindness and the human spirit's ability to endure.

When I was released, I carried these lessons with me. I realized that helping others was not just something I did in prison to survive—it was a calling. I felt compelled to continue reaching out, to share my story, and to support those who were still suffering under the weight of persecution. I started to volunteer with communities in the US that supported human rights and advocated for the freedom of political prisoners, and I volunteered for more than 19 years, facilitating the assimilation of immigrants from the Oromia State of Ethiopia into the American workforce and culture. I knew that my experience had given me a unique perspective, and I wanted to use it to make a difference in the world.

My relationship with Danny deepened as well. The bond we formed during our imprisonment became an unbreakable foundation for our future. We had survived the worst together, and now we were determined to build a life that honored the strength and resilience we had discovered in ourselves and each other. Despite the physical scars we carried, we knew that our love and commitment to one another were stronger than ever.

RESILIENCE

Me and my husband Danny

As I look back on my time in prison, I no longer see it as a period of defeat or despair. Instead, I see it as a period of transformation— a time when I was tested, challenged, and ultimately strengthened. The fire of persecution had tried to consume me, but like the mythical Phoenix, I rose from the ashes, renewed and reborn.

And now, as I share my story with you, I hope it will serve as a testament to the power of resilience, faith, and the unbreakable human spirit. There is always hope, no matter how dark the circumstances or how deep the pain is. There is always a way to rise from the ashes and find the strength to continue forward.

Chapter 4
Community Resilience

Section I: Support Systems

Resilience is not something one builds in isolation; rather, it is nurtured by the shared experiences we live through, by the collective strength of those around us, and by the unwavering support of others who offer their hands when we can no longer stand alone. Hardships have a way of drawing out our deepest vulnerabilities, but it's often the people around us—whether family, friends or even strangers—who step in to catch us when we fall. These acts of kindness, no matter how small they may seem in the moment, leave lasting imprints on our hearts. They become the scaffolding that holds us together when we are most at risk of falling apart. Through all the challenges I have faced, I have been blessed with a network of individuals who have carried me through my darkest moments. This chapter is also dedicated to the countless acts of support that have illuminated my path, not out of duty but out of love and shared responsibility. The stories that follow illustrate how community and culture have been lifelines, interweaving threads of connection and hope that have bound me to the people who refused to let me walk alone.

One of the most painful and trying periods of my life was my imprisonment in Ethiopia. This time was defined by deep uncertainty, fear, and a profound sense of isolation. The cold, unyielding stone walls of Ma'kalawi prison held me captive, not just physically but emotionally, as the weight of my circumstances seemed impossible to bear. Yet, even in the darkest moments of that confinement, I wasn't completely abandoned. My family, especially my sister Million and my uncle Dr. Mekonen, took it upon themselves to ensure that I was provided for in ways that the prison system failed to do. My mother lived far away and couldn't physically be there, but Million and Uncle Dr. Mekonen bridged that gap. They made arrangements for meals to be delivered to me daily from a nearby restaurant. While some might view a meal as a simple necessity, in the grim reality of prison life, it was so much more. Each meal served as a reminder of the world beyond those walls, a lifeline connecting me to the people who loved me. It was more than sustenance—it was a symbol of care, a reminder that I had not been forgotten and that my existence still held meaning. The consistency of their support became a balm for my weary soul, easing the mental and emotional strain that imprisonment inflicted upon me. The food they sent wasn't just nourishment for my body; it was the message of their love and the strength they lent me each day, a force that kept me going.

What touched me deeply during this period was the fact that support came from beyond the walls of my family. There is one act of kindness that still brings me to tears, even now—a gesture from someone who could have easily ignored my plight. A former Minister of Agriculture in Ethiopia, a man I had only briefly met through my husband, reached out during my time of need. Despite the fact that we were not close, this prominent figure saw my suffering and extended his hand by sending financial support. It wasn't about the money itself—though it was certainly helpful—but what moved me was the message behind it. His gesture whispered, "I see you. You are not invisible. Your life has worth." In a time when I felt powerless, when my very existence seemed to be fading into the shadows of those prison walls, his kindness was like a beacon. It illuminated the dark space I was in, reminding me that even those in positions of power saw my humanity and chose to act. It wasn't just a financial gift; it was an affirmation that I still mattered, that my life had value, even when I felt forgotten by the world.

But the kindness I experienced didn't stop there. My classmates, Kelemwerk Tekle and Selamawit Lema, even without knowing the full scope of my arrest, showed me a depth of friendship that I had never fully appreciated until that moment. Two of my school friends made sure that I was never without food. They alternated days, bringing me extra food or sharing their own meals so that I wouldn't go hungry. These weren't just small acts of generosity; they were lifelines, a testament to the bond we shared. Through their consistent care, they gave me not only the food I needed to survive but also the emotional support that sustained me. They showed me that even in the face of uncertainty, even when they could have turned away, they chose to stand by me. These friends, once just part of my everyday life, became pillars that I leaned on, and their kindness reminded me that I had not been forgotten.

RESILIENCE

Inside the prison, the support continued, not just from those on the outside but from my fellow prisoners. A university student, Sahilu, who was imprisoned for being a suspected member of the Eritrean People's Liberation Front, Ms. Genet Mebratu, who was imprisoned because her husband, General Merid Nigussie, opposed the government, extended a gesture that touched me deeply. She took a personal risk by giving me a Bible, a simple yet profound act of kindness. In those pages, I found strength, hope, and a connection to my faith that helped carry me through some of the most difficult moments. Other women in the prison also supported me in ways that may seem small but were monumental in that environment. Many of them took it upon themselves to wash my clothes, sparing me from one of the many indignities of prison life. While washing clothes might seem like a minor chore, in that space, it was an act of solidarity, a recognition that we were all in this together. These women, who had their own burdens to carry, chose to lift mine as well, and their compassion made the unbearable a little more bearable.

Opening our home to those in need became a natural extension of the values my family instilled in me. Just as my family rallied around me during my imprisonment, we welcomed those who had nowhere else to turn. It wasn't just about offering shelter—it was about creating a safe space for individuals to grow and rebuild their lives. When I moved to the United States, this sense of community carried over. My family and I opened our doors to refugees—people from all walks of life, regardless of their religion or background.

Some lived with us for a year, others for two years or just six months, but no matter the length of their stay, we made sure they felt supported and cared for. We welcomed people of different faiths—Muslims, Orthodox believers, and Protestants alike—because, to us, it wasn't about religion. It was about humanity, about showing love and compassion to those in need. I'll never forget one particular situation where we took in a man who was HIV-positive, unaware of his condition until later. We provided him and his 8-year-old son with shelter over the weekends, comforted him, and eventually encouraged him to reunite with his family before his condition worsened. He passed away shortly after, but I know that the time he spent with us made a difference in his final days.

Opening our home wasn't without its challenges, but it shaped who I am today. It showed me that resilience isn't just something we develop through our own struggles; it's something we nurture in others. By offering a safe haven to those who have suffered, we help them rediscover their own strength.

Support also came from my husband's comrades, who found ways to remind me that I wasn't alone, even when I felt most isolated. People like Mulugata Mosisa, Nagari Fayisa, Obbo Adam Jilo, Eshetu Letu, Musa'e Tesfatsion, and Hadish played pivotal roles in helping me stay strong. I remember how Obbo Adam Jilo would sit in the sun, positioning himself so that I could see him when I walked to the interrogator's office and how supportive prisoners ran to the edges of their prison to see me and show me their support. It was their way of sending me a silent message, a reminder that I was not forgotten, that there were people waiting for me on the other side of those walls. There was also a comrade who gave me a pair of socks during the freezing nights. Those socks weren't just about physical warmth; they were about emotional warmth, too. In those harsh conditions, they reminded me that I was still cared for and that even on the coldest of nights, there were people looking out for me. These acts of kindness from my husband's comrades were not just about survival—they were about maintaining my dignity, about helping me remember that I was still part of a community, still part of something larger than myself.

Faith and community were intertwined throughout this period, providing a source of strength that carried me when I couldn't carry myself. I was fortunate to have friends from different religious backgrounds—Christian, Muslim, and non-religious—who supported me without hesitation. In those moments, the divisions that sometimes separate us fell away, and what remained was our shared humanity. These friends, regardless of their beliefs, became a source of comfort and belonging, showing me that when we come together, we are stronger than we ever could be alone.

Before my imprisonment, I had already experienced the power of community in my family gatherings. Every Sunday, we would gather at my grandfather's house, where the warmth of family filled the air. It was a sanctuary from the world's troubles, a place where I could feel safe, loved, and connected. My uncle, aunt, sisters and I, many of whom were close in age, would play together in a beautiful front yard with flowers, Apple trees and Coffee plants, forming bonds that would carry us through the hardest of times. It was in those moments that I first learned the importance of collective support, a lesson that has remained with me through every chapter of my life.

When I moved back from Nekemte to Finfinne (Addis Ababa) and joined music school, I faced a daunting transition, but once again, I was met with unwavering support. My uncle, Ayele Jaalata, gave me a place to stay, ensuring that I had a roof over my head while I pursued my education. My sister Serawit and her ex-husband Zelelw, even after moving to Dire Dawa, continued to provide me with financial assistance and let me move to their house in Bole, making sure that I could focus on my studies without worrying about how I would meet my basic needs. These gestures, though perhaps unnoticed by the outside world, were pivotal in shaping my ability to persevere. They reinforced the lesson that has guided me throughout my life: survival is never a solitary endeavor—it is always a collective one.

Section II: Collective Strength:

In every culture, there exists a deep-rooted belief in the strength that arises when a community comes together, bound by shared responsibility. This collective strength is what has allowed me, and so many others, to rise above hardships that would otherwise have been too much to bear.

The strength of my own community was something I witnessed firsthand during the most difficult times. The Dado tradition, practiced by Oromo women, is a shining example of how deeply embedded this sense of shared responsibility is in our culture. When one woman is in need, the others rally to her side, sharing resources, offering emotional support, and helping with the burdens of daily life. The Dado system ensures that no woman faces her struggles alone. In these moments, the true strength of my culture is revealed as women come together to lift one another up.

Another significant tradition that embodies this collective strength is Dabaree, where wealthier farmers lend female livestock to poorer households. This act ensures that those less fortunate have access to milk and a livelihood. The firstborn calf is passed on to another family in need, creating a cycle of generosity that uplifts not just individuals but entire communities. This reciprocal relationship weaves a bond of solidarity that transcends individual survival. It's not just about one person making it through—it's about ensuring that everyone has a chance to thrive. These practices, deeply rooted in tradition, have saved lives and nurtured a profound sense of interdependence. The support network I received during my imprisonment mirrored these cultural practices, as people offered what they could, not out of obligation, but out of love and shared humanity.

When my husband and I faced the challenges of adapting to life in the United States, we were once again reminded of the power of collective strength. Upon our arrival, my brother-in-law, Samuel Daffa, opened his home to us. His generosity gave us the stability we desperately needed in those early days. Living with Samuel wasn't just about having a place to stay—it was about knowing that we had someone in our corner, someone who would guide us as we navigated this new reality. It was in those moments that I realized community extends far beyond blood ties. It is built through shared experiences, mutual understanding, and a deep sense of responsibility to one another.

I have seen firsthand how these cultural practices of collective strength can transform lives. The work of my organization, C.G. Women's Empowerment (CGWE), is deeply influenced by these cultural practices. I will discuss about my organization in detail in the next chapter.

Also, this sense of community became even more pronounced during the COVID-19 pandemic. My husband and I both contracted the virus, and the physical and emotional toll it took on us was immense. Yet, once again, we found ourselves surrounded by a community that refused to let us face the situation alone. Friends, family, and church members rallied around us, dropping off groceries and meals at our doorstep. Their kindness wasn't just about providing sustenance—it was about making sure we knew we were cared for, even in isolation. These small acts of compassion lifted our spirits when we were at our weakest, reminding us that we were not alone.

After we recovered, we felt an obligation to pay forward the kindness we had received. We knew firsthand how isolating and frightening the virus could be, so we made it a point to help others who were quarantined, especially those far from home. We prayed, delivered groceries, and meals to friends, clients, and even strangers who were stuck in hotels or Airbnb rentals, separated from their families. It was our way of extending the love and support that had been shown to us, ensuring that others knew they, too, mattered.

As I reflect on these moments of collective strength and support, I am reminded that resilience is not just about individual survival. It is about the connections we forge, the hands we hold, and the love we share along the way. The people who stood by me in my darkest hours, who fed me, clothed me, prayed for me, and reminded me of my worth, were not just helping me endure—they were helping me rise. In the face of overwhelming hardship, it was community, faith, and culture that became my lifeline. And as I continue my journey, I carry with me the lessons they taught me: that no challenge is insurmountable when we come together, that we are stronger in unity, and that, in lifting others, we all rise. My story, like so many others, is a proof that while the road may be difficult, we are never truly alone. Together, we can overcome anything.

Chapter 5
Empowering Others

Section I: Women and Children

The fight for empowerment, for dignity, and for the right to be seen begins at home, in the small, intimate spaces where our most formative experiences unfold. For me, it all started with my mother, whose quiet strength and relentless determination shaped my understanding of the power we all hold to make a difference in the world. My mother didn't just combat harmful traditional practices in our community—she lived her life as a beacon of hope, illuminating the path forward for those who followed her. Her life embodied the scripture: "In the same way, let your light shine before others, that they may see your good deeds and glorify your Father in heaven" (Matthew 5:16). Her journey wasn't without difficulty, but it was precisely those hardships that taught her to stand firm, not only for herself but for other women and children who were facing similar challenges.

In Oromia, Ethiopia, harmful practices like early marriage, female genital mutilation (FGM), and gender-based violence were everyday realities. These practices, ingrained in tradition, had devastating consequences for women and girls, stripping them of their autonomy and often condemning them to a lifetime of pain and hardship. My mother, however, (once she got the awareness of harmful traditional practice) of was not one to stand by and let these injustices continue. She understood that fighting such deeply rooted traditions required both courage and compassion. Her approach was never loud or confrontational; instead, she spoke with the quiet conviction of someone who had lived through these struggles herself. She believed that every woman, regardless of her background, had the right to live free from fear, to raise her children in safety, and to make decisions about her own body and life.

It was from my mother that I learned one of the most important lessons in life: to empower others, you must first listen to their stories. The women in our community weren't asking for much. They didn't want luxury or power; they wanted the most basic of human rights—safety for their children, access to education for their daughters, and the freedom to live without the constant threat of violence. Yet, in many parts of Oromia, even these modest requests were often too much to ask.

My mother's fight against these injustices wasn't easy, but it was necessary. I remember her intervening when one of my siblings was at risk of undergoing female genital mutilation. She had learned about the lasting trauma—both physical and emotional—that FGM inflicted on women, and she refused to let her daughters suffer the same fate. It wasn't an easy decision to stand up against the community's expectations, but my mother did it with love and courage. In doing so, she not only saved my sibling from a harmful practice but also set an example for other women in the community, showing them that it was possible to say no to protect their daughters from these damaging traditions.

Beyond her activism, my mother was also a woman of great resourcefulness. With the support of her brother, Gebeyehou, she was able to attend Singer Sewing School in Finfinnee (Addis Ababa). This opportunity empowered her, giving her the skills and confidence to support herself and her family. She learned how to sew and soon became a master of her craft. My mother would often sit with catalogs, picking out designs that caught her eye, then meticulously creating patterns and sewing dresses for us. I still remember those beautiful garments, the pride in her work, and the joy it brought her to see her children wearing clothes she had made with her own hands.

Some of the dresses my mom sewed for us.
Left to right, my sister Million, my aunt Ababye, my sister Serawit and me (Mimi) on the right corner.

RESILIENCE

Sewing became more than just a means of providing for her family—it became a symbol of empowerment. Through her sewing, my mother saved money that would have otherwise been spent on clothing, and she also earned an income by teaching other women in the community and orphans in missionary compounds how to sew. With the income generated from sewing, she was able to pay for her children's school at a Lutheran private school to get a better education until the time the government took the church's properties.

But my mother wasn't the only woman in my life who taught me the power of empowerment through action. My grandmother, too, played a pivotal role in shaping my understanding of community and care. She owned cows and Coffee farms. Those cows and income from Coffee beans became the lifeblood of our household. My grandmother used their milk to make yogurt and butter, which sustained us. We enjoyed drinking the grass-fed cow milk, and she even used the cow dung as fertilizer for her garden. She also sold one of the bulls to send my sibling for better education in the capital city of Finfinnee (Addis Ababa). The cow, though just an animal, was a source of nourishment, security, and even joy. As children, we adored the calves, especially the newborn ones. We treated them like pets, playing with them, laughing as they trotted around the yard, their big eyes full of innocence and wonder.

These simple joys—like playing with the calves—were a reminder that empowerment isn't always grand or monumental. Sometimes, it's found in the everyday acts of care and kindness that keep a family fed and clothed.

Faith played an integral role in my family's journey of resilience. It was through faith that my mother and grandmother found the strength to continue, even when the odds seemed insurmountable. My mother's actions always reflected her faith in something greater, aligning with Proverbs 19:17, which reminds us: *"Whoever is kind to the poor lends to the LORD, and he will reward them for what they have done."*

Faith has also been a constant source of strength in my personal journey. During times of hardship, when the weight of the challenges before me felt overwhelming, my faith grounded me. It gave me the courage to continue, even when it seemed easier to give up. The work of C.G. Women's Empowerment (CGWE) is deeply rooted in this same faith. Our belief in the inherent dignity and worth of every individual is the foundation of our mission. Over the years, our partnerships with the local Non-Governmental Organization (NGO) Hundee Oromo Grassroots Development Initiative, which plans to facilitate the implementation of the proposed project aimed at enhancing the livelihoods of resource-poor and highly marginalized women, have been crucial. Hundee also monitors and evaluates project activities in close consultation and collaboration with key stakeholders, relevant government partners, and community elders in Oromia. Additionally, Rotary Clubs and churches have been instrumental in supporting our work. Churches such as the Oromia Evangelical Church in Nekemte, with spiritual encouragement in the communities and support CGWE volunteer mission trip travelers from the US interpreting Oromo language and English during trainings/workshops and New Life Church in the United States have played a vital role in both financial support and spiritual encouragement. Additionally, New Albany Catholic Church of the Resurrection has extended their help by supplying clothes to new beneficiaries, ensuring that both the physical and spiritual needs of the community are met. This holistic approach has had a profound impact, allowing people to not only receive material assistance but also grow in their faith with a message they can fully understand.

Members of these churches, fellow Rotarians, and other CGWE supporters have traveled to Oromia, Ethiopia, on mission trips, witnessing firsthand the impact of CGWE's work and contributing directly to the cause. These partnerships have been more than transactional—they've been transformative, reinforcing the belief that we are all connected, bound by a shared responsibility to uplift one another. Importantly, this support has not been limited to faith-based communities. People of various beliefs and backgrounds, including those outside the Christian faith, have come together in solidarity, joining hands to rescue, empower, and uplift the most vulnerable. Their collective efforts have allowed CGWE to expand its reach and impact, providing a moral compass that transcends religious boundaries and continues to guide our work. It's a testament to the power of humanity when we come together, united by a common goal to bring hope and change.

It was this spirit of collective care and responsibility that extended into our broader community. In our culture, there is a tradition called Dabo, where neighbors come together to help one another during the farming and harvest seasons. These gatherings were not only about getting the work done—they were about building bonds of trust and solidarity. During times of famine or hardship, Dabo was a lifeline, ensuring that no family was left to fend for themselves. Everyone shared in the labor, and everyone shared in the harvest.

This tradition of mutual support carried over even when our community migrated to the diaspora. Here, far from our homeland, we continued to support one another. When someone was sick and couldn't afford medical bills, the community would rally to help. When a family member passed away, we would come together to raise the money needed for burial expenses, even helping to transport the body back home if necessary. In these acts of solidarity, we carried with us the values we had learned from our mothers and grandmothers—the values of care, community, and mutual support. This aligns closely with 1 Timothy 5:3-8, which calls on us to *"Take care of widows who are destitute."*

It was these same values that shaped the founding of C.G. Women's Empowerment (CGWE) in 2012. Inspired by the lessons of my mother and grandmother, I wanted to create an organization that would empower women and children in Oromia by providing them with the tools they needed to break free from cycles of poverty and violence. I witnessed the freedom women have in this country

RESILIENCE

(US) and decided to fulfill my passion and dedication to empower women in my birthplace (Oromia) by creating this non-profit organization. Our mission is simple: to create economic self-sufficiency for women and children, to ensure their safety from violence and discrimination, and to empower them to build better futures for themselves.

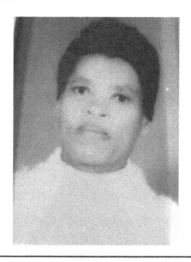

Guuttatta Cawwaaqee

That's how CGWE was born. CGWE stands for Cawwaaqee Guuttatta Women's Empowerment. The organization is named in honor of Cawwaaqee Guuttatta, my grandmother, who endured a life of immense hardship. Forced into marriage against her will, Cawwaaqee had no opportunity to stand up for herself and was left with no choice but to persevere through challenging circumstances. She walked 10-15 kilometers (6-9 miles) to reach her distant farm fields, where she grew coffee beans and corn to sell, providing for her family. Despite these struggles, she managed the household's needs, ensuring her children and her grandchildren were well-fed with products from her cow, such as milk, butter, and yogurt.

The first initiative we, the CGWE board of director, launched was modeled after an old Oromo tradition called Dabaree, a practice of sharing resources within the community. In Dabaree, wealthier farmers would lend a cow to poorer families, allowing them access to milk and dairy products. The idea was that when the cow gave birth, the family would pass on the firstborn calf to another family in need, creating a self-sustaining cycle of support and empowerment.

Happy women receiving cows through the Dabaree program

RESILIENCE

One of the women who benefitted from Dabaree was Dasse Fite, a widow and mother of three. Before receiving a cow from CGWE, Dasse was struggling to provide for her children. She couldn't afford to send them to school, and she feared for their future. But with the cow, her life began to change. The cow provided milk for her children, and Dasse was able to sell the surplus, generating income that allowed her to send her children to school and improve her home. Her transformation was more than just financial—it was personal. She regained her sense of dignity, and she became an example for other women in her community, showing them that it was possible to rise above their circumstances.

Dasse's story is just one of many. Since 2012, CGWE has started with 3 cows and provided over 610 cows to women in Oromia, directly impacting more than 3,600 individuals. More than 300 cows gave birth, and more than 70 women gave their firstborn calves to women in the communities. Each woman who receives a cow agrees to pass on the firstborn calf to another woman, continuing the cycle of empowerment and hope. This model of reciprocity has created a ripple effect, transforming entire communities by giving women the means to provide for their families with dignity and independence.

Dasse and her daughter with their cows.

Another powerful story is that of Alemi Wagari, a mother who once felt so hopeless that she considered taking her own life. Alemi had several children to care for but no means to provide for them. She was at her lowest point when she became a CGWE beneficiary. After receiving a cow, Alemi's life began to change. The cow provided milk for her children, and Alemi was able to sell the excess, generating enough income to start rebuilding her life. Today, Alemi owns five cows and has become a leader in her community, mentoring other women and showing them that with support and determination, anything is possible.

Alemi Wagari, her kids and her cows.

RESILIENCE

These stories of transformation are the foundation of our mission at CGWE. Our goal has always been to empower women and children by giving them the tools they need to succeed. Whether it's through providing cows, solar lights, or educational materials, our aim is always to break the cycle of poverty and create lasting change in the lives of the most vulnerable.

In addition to Dabaree, we also strengthen Dado system. This system brings women together to support one another, whether through sharing resources, offering emotional support, or helping with day-to-day tasks. No woman should have to face her challenges alone, and Dado ensures that there is always a network of care and support for those who need it most.

Through these programs, we have seen families grow stronger, children thrive in school, and women take on leadership roles they never thought possible. And yet, our work is far from finished.

As we continued our work with CGWE, it became clear that education was one of the most powerful tools we could offer. For many women and children in Oromia, access to education was severely limited, not only by poverty but also by traditional gender roles that often relegated women and girls to the home, depriving them of the opportunity to learn and grow. We knew that breaking the cycle of poverty would require more than just financial support—it would require a fundamental shift in how women and children viewed themselves and their futures.

Our first step was to establish reading corners in local schools, providing children with access to books and educational materials that they otherwise wouldn't have. Over the years, these reading corners have reached more than 4,300 children, giving them the tools they need to succeed in school and beyond. The impact has been remarkable. Before the introduction of these reading corners, many of the children in our program struggled to keep up with their studies, often falling behind because they lacked the resources to continue learning outside of school hours.

One of the biggest barriers to education in Oromia was the lack of electricity. In all villages, children couldn't study after dark because their homes had no lighting. This was especially challenging for students who needed to complete homework or study for exams. To address this, we introduced solar lights to the communities we serve, distributing more than 1,300 solar light bulbs to families in need. These lights were a game-changer for the children and their families, allowing them to extend their learning time well into the evening.

These solar lights, like the cows we distribute through Dabaree, represent opportunities for change, breaking through the limitations imposed by poverty."—When I think of many other children whose lives have been transformed by something as simple as a light bulb, I am reminded that the smallest actions can have the greatest impact.

RESILIENCE

A child smiling after receiving a solar light bulb. In addition to providing educational tools and resources, we also understood that creating a supportive and thriving community meant addressing the broader needs of the families we served. Education was only one part of the solution. The health and well-being of these families were just as critical in ensuring that they could thrive. Many of the communities we worked with lacked access to basic necessities like clean drinking water and healthcare, both of which were fundamental to breaking the cycle of poverty.

Providing treatment Shanna Huber nurse practitioner, Zelalem Desalegn public health professional, Tirunesh Beyene nurse practitioner, Terri Kirk, Connie Kirk, Brenda Floyd and Mimi for elephantiasis, educating on personal hygiene, and addressing female genital mutilation (FGM).

To address these challenges, CGWE partnered with local and international organizations like Rotary Clubs to build three wells in remote villages, providing clean water to families who had previously walked miles just to collect water. The impact of these wells has been profound, particularly for women and children, who often bore the brunt of the responsibility for fetching water. Before the wells were constructed, women would spend hours walking to the nearest water source, leaving little time for them to engage in other productive activities. Children were deeply affected as well, with many missing school to help their mothers fetch water or due to waterborne illnesses caused by bacteria, viruses, or parasites contaminating the water supply. These diseases didn't just impact the children; adults, too, were forced to miss work, while the elderly, particularly vulnerable to waterborne diseases, often found themselves unable to continue their daily responsibilities.

One of the other critical initiatives we introduced was providing a two-day long training on good animal husbandry practices and fodder development. In addition to that we constructed a village veterinary clinic. This clinic was vital in ensuring that the cows and other livestock that families depended on for their livelihoods remained healthy. Healthy cows meant stable families, and by providing veterinary care, we were able to help these families maintain their economic stability.

I still remember the day the first village veterinary clinic opened. There was a palpable sense of excitement and relief in the air. Families who had been struggling with sick animals now had a place to bring them for treatment. The clinic quickly became a cornerstone of the community, ensuring that the cows and other livestock remained healthy and productive. The impact of this initiative went beyond just improving the health of the animals—it gave the community a sense of security, knowing that they had access to the resources they needed to protect their livelihoods.

As we continued to expand our initiatives, one of the most rewarding aspects of our work was seeing how the women who had once been beneficiaries of our programs were now becoming leaders in their own right. Many of these women, after receiving a cow through the Dabaree program (reciprocity), went on to pass their firstborn calves on to other women, continuing the cycle of giving and empowerment. This wasn't just about charity—it was about creating a self-sustaining system where women could uplift one another and build stronger, more resilient communities.

RESILIENCE

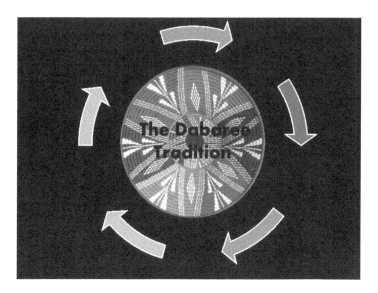

The ripple effect is something we see time and again in the work we do. Women who were once marginalized, economically disenfranchised, and trapped in cycles of poverty are now leaders in their communities, lifting others as they themselves have been lifted. The success of CGWE's initiatives goes beyond just the numbers—it's about the lasting change we're creating in the lives of these women, their families, and their communities.

Section II: Broader Impact

The impact of CGWE's work is not just confined to individual success stories like those of Dasse and Alemi. Our initiatives have created a broader societal shift, changing the way communities view women's roles and capabilities. The work we started in 2012 with the simple goal of empowering women and children has since evolved into a movement that is transforming entire communities, both socially and economically.

In addition to the Dabaree program, CGWE and Hundee, the local partner, have also introduced Self-Help Groups (SHGs), where women come together to support one another, learn basic small-business skills, and collectively save money. These SHGs have become a vital part of the communities we serve, fostering both financial independence and social solidarity. In a region where women often lack access to formal banking systems, these groups have provided a safe space for women to save money and access small loans, which they can use to start businesses or improve their homes.

One of the most powerful aspects of the SHG model is the sense of empowerment and self-reliance it fosters. Women who had previously been dependent on others for their survival are now in control of their own financial futures. The average weekly savings of women in these groups ranges from 10 to 20 Birr (approximately $0.18 to $0.35), and while these amounts may seem small, they represent a significant step toward financial independence for these women. Collectively, the women in our SHGs have saved over

921,600 Birr (approximately $16,168), which they have used to invest in their families, their homes, and their businesses.

The SHG model has also helped to create a sense of community and belonging among the women involved. In many cases, these women had previously been isolated, either because of their economic circumstances or because of the traditional gender roles that kept them confined to their homes. But through the SHGs, they have found a network of support, both financial and emotional, that has given them the confidence to take control of their lives and their futures.

A heartfelt moment capturing how these women in the SHG were there for each other both emotionally and financially.

One of the women who has benefited from the SHG model is Yadatee, who was on the verge of giving up hope before she joined the group. Yadatee had struggled for years to provide for her family, and she felt as though she had no way out. But through the SHG, she not only gained access to financial resources but also found a community of women who supported her, encouraged her, and helped her see that she wasn't alone in her struggles. Today, Yadatee is providing for her family and helping other women in her community by sharing her story and mentoring them as they navigate their own challenges.

In addition to the SHGs, CGWE has also made significant strides in improving access to education for children in the communities we serve. As mentioned earlier, our reading corners and solar lights have had a transformative impact on the academic performance of thousands of children. The results speak for themselves: in one district, 68% of 8th graders who used our reading corners passed the National 8th Grade Exam, compared to just 20% in private schools.

Students in one of the reading corners.

RESILIENCE

Faith continues to be at the core of our work. The partnerships we've built with churches have not only supported our programs financially but have also nurtured the spirit of the communities we serve. Beyond providing resources, these partnerships offer hope and spiritual encouragement. As the Proverbs 31:20 verse says, *"She opens her arms to the poor and extends her hands to the needy."* This encapsulates what we aim to achieve at CGWE. We open our arms to those in need and extend our hands to help lift them.

Looking ahead, the future of CGWE is filled with promise. Our goal is to continue providing 60 cows per year, impacting an additional 360 individuals annually. If funding permits, we purchase more than 60 cows annually as CGWE continues to expand its efforts to empower women in rural Oromia. We are also committed to expanding our reading corners in schools and continuing to provide solar light bulbs to families in need. Our long-term vision includes working on mobile animal clinics to reach out to remote areas and exploring innovative solutions such as artificial insemination to increase livestock productivity and help women further grow their herds.

But beyond the numbers, beyond the statistics, the true measure of our success is the hope we see in the eyes of the women and children we serve. Hope for a better future, hope for a life free from the chains of poverty and oppression. This hope is what drives us forward, what fuels our mission to empower others.

When I look back on the journey that has brought us here, I am filled with a deep sense of gratitude and purpose. I envision a future where the work we have started continues to inspire generations to come, where the lessons of resilience, perseverance, and dedication to the human cause are passed down to those who will follow in our footsteps.

For future generations, I want my story and the stories of the women we have empowered to serve as a guide. Life will always be filled with challenges, but it is through these challenges that we find our strength. I want future generations to know that no matter how insurmountable the odds may seem, they have the power within themselves to overcome. The path may not always be easy, but it is through perseverance, faith, and a commitment to lifting others that we can navigate the ups and downs of life.

My hope is that the future leaders of our communities will continue the work we have started, building on the foundation of empowerment, compassion, and collective responsibility that we have laid. I envision a world where every woman and child has the opportunity to thrive, where the cycles of poverty and violence are broken, and where hope is not just a dream but a reality for all.

Faith, love, and community have always been our guiding forces, and as we move forward, they will continue to be the pillars upon which CGWE stands. Together, with our partners, supporters, and the women we serve, we will keep pushing toward a brighter, more empowered future for all.

RESILIENCE

Chapter 6
From Local Heroes to Global Advocates

Section I: Grassroots Movements and Sustainable Development

The story of advocacy and empowerment is not just one of facts and milestones; it is a deeply emotional journey woven with the threads of personal sacrifice, resilience, and unwavering commitment to a cause greater than oneself. For me, the road to global advocacy began in the intimate spaces of my own community, where oppression was not an abstract concept but a daily reality. The seeds of this journey were planted in the soil of hardship and watered by the collective will of my people to rise above their circumstances.

I remember the early 1990s in Oromia, Ethiopia—a time when fear was a constant companion. My people were being violently evicted from their homes, stripped of their lands, and left to face an uncertain future. It was as if a dark cloud had descended over us, suffocating our hopes and dreams. Families were torn apart, and the sense of helplessness was palpable. Yet, even in the midst of this turmoil, there was a spark—a small but powerful glimmer of resistance. It was in these moments of despair that I realized my calling: to stand up, to fight back, and to be a voice for those who had been silenced.

The early grassroots movements I was part of were not driven by grand visions or lofty ideals. They were born out of necessity—a response to the brutality we faced on a daily basis. The Ethiopian military regime's oppressive tactics were designed to break our spirits, to make us believe that we had no power. But we did have power. And that power came from our unity, our shared pain, and our collective determination to resist. I joined the Oromo movement because I could no longer stand by and watch my people suffer. The fight for our rights was not just a political struggle; it was a moral imperative. We were fighting for our dignity, our land, and our right to exist.

One of the most emotionally charged moments of this movement was seeing the strength of the women in my community. Despite the violence and uncertainty, they stood tall, refusing to be broken by the circumstances. These women—many of whom had lost their homes, their husbands, and even their children—became the backbone of our resistance. They reminded me that empowerment does not begin in political arenas or boardrooms; it begins in the hearts of individuals who refuse to give up. Watching them fight for their families, their land, and their dignity ignited a fire within me—a fire that would later shape the work I would do for the rest of my life.

Years later, after immigrating to the United States, the fire that had been kindled in Oromia continued to burn. But the context was different. I was now in a new country, far from the land of my birth, but the challenges of injustice and marginalization remained. The Oromo immigrants I worked with in the U.S. were struggling to find their place in a foreign society. They faced language barriers, cultural dislocation, and economic instability. I saw the same look of uncertainty in their eyes that I had seen in the eyes of my people back in Oromia. But I also saw something else: resilience.

Helping Oromo immigrants integrate into American society was not just about providing them with practical support like job placement or language classes. It was about helping them rediscover their sense of identity and purpose. I saw my role as not just a facilitator but as someone who could help them reignite the fire of resilience within themselves. The work we started in the mid-1990s, creating support networks and preserving cultural traditions, was more than just community service—it was about survival. It was about holding on to who we were while adapting to a new environment.

In 2009, my journey took a transformative turn during a conversation with Mr. Zegeye Asfaw, the former Minister of Agriculture in Ethiopia and founder of the Hundee Grassroots Movement. His vision and passion for empowering the Oromo people deeply resonated with me, and that encounter opened the door to one of the most meaningful chapters of my life. Alongside my husband, we discussed the freedom we are exercising in US, the pressing need to empower women and children in rural Oromia. But this was not just a discussion about logistics or strategy; it was a deeply personal conversation about the pain and struggles of our people and our shared responsibility to do something about it.

We knew that the challenges facing the women and children in Oromia were not going to be solved overnight. The poverty, gender-based violence, and lack of education were deeply entrenched issues that would require a long-term, sustainable approach. But we also knew that we had to act. And so, the C.G. Women's Empowerment (CGWE) nonprofit organization was born—not out of a desire for recognition or accolades but out of a deep, emotional commitment to making a difference.

The Dabaree program, our flagship initiative, was more than just a practical solution to economic instability—it was an expression of our belief in the power of women to transform their communities. The concept was simple: provide women with cows, and they would be able to generate income, feed their families, and create a cycle of giving by passing on the firstborn calf to another woman. But the true power of this program lay in the emotional connections it fostered. The women who participated in Dabaree were not just receiving cows—they were receiving hope. They were being told, in no uncertain terms, that they mattered, that their lives and their contributions were valuable.

One of the most emotional moments for me came when I witnessed a woman who had been struggling to provide for her children, who was about to commit suicide, finally receive her cow. Her tears of gratitude were not just for the physical gift but for what it represented: a chance not to kill herself, to break free from the cycle of poverty and to reclaim her dignity. This moment encapsulated everything that Phoenix Resilience is about—the idea that no matter how many times we are beaten down, we have the power to rise again, stronger than before.

Phoenix Resilience is not just a metaphor; it is a lived reality for the women and children in Oromia who have faced unimaginable hardships but have refused to give up. The stories of these women—women who have overcome violence, poverty, and social marginalization—are the heart of CGWE's mission. Every time I hear their stories, I am reminded of the emotional depth of this work. Empowerment is not just about giving someone a cow or a solar light; it's about giving them the belief that they are capable of shaping their own future.

Our grassroots movements, though deeply rooted in the local context of Oromia, have always had a broader vision. We knew that the work we were doing had the potential to create ripples far beyond the borders of Ethiopia. This is why we placed such a strong emphasis on sustainable development. We didn't want to create temporary fixes to long-standing problems; we wanted to build systems that would continue to empower women and children for generations to come.

RESILIENCE

The Dabaree program, the reading corners in schools, and the solar light initiatives were all designed with this long-term vision in mind. And the results have been more profound than we could have imagined. Since the introduction of reading corners, over 4,300 children have been given the tools they need to succeed academically. But the impact goes beyond the numbers. These initiatives have given children in Oromia something far more valuable: a sense of possibility. They no longer see education as something unattainable or reserved for the privileged; they see it as a pathway to a better future.

This emotional transformation—from despair to hope, from helplessness to empowerment—is the essence of Phoenix Resilience. It's the idea that no matter how many obstacles are placed in our path, we can always find a way to rise above them. It's the belief that even in the darkest of times, there is always a light waiting to be kindled.

As we continue our work in Oromia, we are constantly reminded of the emotional depth of this journey. Every woman who receives a cow, every child who picks up a book in a reading corner, and every family that is able to keep their lights on after dark is a testament to the power of resilience. And this resilience is not just about survival—it's about thriving, about creating a future full of hope, dignity, and possibility.

Section II: Scaling Local Initiatives for Global Change

As the work of CGWE expanded, so did the emotional stakes. What began as a grassroots movement in Oromia, driven by the immediate needs of my people, soon grew into a global advocacy effort. The challenges we addressed in Oromia—economic instability, lack of education, gender-based violence—were not unique to our region. These were global challenges that required global solutions.

RESILIENCE

The emotional toll of this realization was immense. While we had made significant strides in Oromia, the knowledge that so many other communities around the world were facing similar struggles was both heartbreaking and galvanizing. It became clear to us that the model we had developed in Oromia—the combination of grassroots empowerment and sustainable development—had the potential to create lasting change in other regions as well.

Scaling our local initiatives to a global level required more than just logistical planning; it required a deep emotional commitment to the idea that every life we touched had the potential to create a ripple effect of empowerment. The work we had done in Oromia, particularly through the Dabaree program, had shown us that even small actions—like giving a woman a cow—could have profound, far-reaching impacts. And so, we began to look for ways to replicate this model in other parts of the world.

Our partnerships with international NGOs, advocacy groups, and faith-based organizations became crucial in this effort. These partnerships were not just about pooling resources or sharing best practices; they were about creating a global community of advocates united by a shared vision of empowerment and resilience. Through these partnerships, we were able to take the lessons we had learned in Oromia and apply them on a global stage.

Members of the Church, NGOs and individuals have traveled back to Ethiopia on mission trips, providing hands-on support and sharing their expertise in areas like education, health, and agriculture. These trips have not only strengthened the bond but have also created opportunities for cross-cultural exchange and learning. The emotional depth of these trips cannot be overstated.

Oromia evangelical church elders and Wollaga University instructors who were closely connected to the struggles in Oromia continue volunteering and supporting us. They were inspired by our motto and worked hard to make a difference for the mothers, students, and families of our very poor church members. Since they couldn't afford to give cows, they gave sheep instead. We became a model for others in Oromia, and they followed our example. Their support—both financial and emotional—has been instrumental in scaling our initiatives and ensuring that the work we do in Oromia continues to thrive. As we scaled our initiatives, the emotional impact of our work became even more apparent. Seeing the model Hundee had developed in Oromia, CGWE being replicated in other regions was a deeply emotional moment for me. It was a testament to the power of Phoenix Resilience—the idea that communities, no matter how oppressed or marginalized, have the ability to rise from the ashes of hardship and create lasting change.

Our education initiatives, particularly the introduction of reading corners and solar lights, have also had a profound global impact. These simple yet powerful tools have transformed the lives of thousands of children, giving them the opportunity to break free from the cycle of poverty and pursue their dreams. The emotional significance of these initiatives cannot be overstated. For many of these children, education was once a distant dream—something they could only imagine. But through our work, that dream has become a reality.

The journey from local activism to global advocacy is one that is filled with both triumphs and challenges. It is a journey that requires not only strategic thinking and planning but also a deep emotional commitment to the cause. At the heart of this journey is the concept of Phoenix Resilience—the belief that no matter how many times we are beaten down, we have the power to rise again, stronger and more determined than before.

Through the work of CGWE, we have seen the power of this resilience firsthand. We have watched as women and children in Oromia, once marginalized and voiceless, have found the strength to stand up and claim their place in the world. We have seen how local initiatives, born out of necessity, can grow into global movements that inspire change on a larger scale. And we have witnessed the emotional transformation that comes from empowering individuals to take control of their own lives.

As we look to the future, we are filled with hope. The work we have done in Oromia has already changed countless lives, and the ripple effect of this work will continue to spread for generations to come. But more than that, we believe that the values of community, collective responsibility, and Phoenix Resilience that have guided us will continue to inspire future generations to push for a more just and equitable world.

Through the lens of emotional depth and resilience, this chapter highlights not only the practical impact of CGWE's initiatives but also the emotional journey of empowerment that has shaped our work and will continue to shape our future. On behalf of CGWE board of directors, I would like to say "Thank You" to all CGWE supporters!

RESILIENCE

Chapter 7
The Final Step

Section I: Reflection on Transformation

As we reach the final chapter of this book, it may seem like the end, but in truth, this is just another beginning. Life is a series of doors opening, even when it feels like every door has been shut. This story, my story, is not one of finality but of continuous growth, of rising again and again, even when it feels like all has been lost. This chapter is not a conclusion but rather a reflection—a moment to breathe, to look back, and to see that every step, every hardship, has led to a greater understanding of myself and the world around me.

When I think back on this journey, I realize that it has not been simply about surviving but about transforming. Each struggle, each moment of despair, every triumph—it has all been part of an ever-evolving story, shaping me into who I am today. The world did not make me stronger; I chose strength in a world that sought to break me. And in that strength, I found resilience. True resilience isn't just about enduring; it's about rising again and again, no matter how many times life knocks you down.

There was a time when I thought I had nothing left to give when

RESILIENCE

the days blurred together in a seemingly endless cycle of pain. I remember standing in a small, dimly lit room, hearing the sound of my own breath, wondering if it would be my last. Torture does that—it forces you to confront not only the limits of your physical body but the fragility of your very existence. I felt stripped of everything, my humanity hanging by a thread. Yet, in that darkness, I discovered something even deeper. A truth I hadn't yet grasped fully: that no amount of physical pain could break the core of who I was.

This wasn't a moment of clarity that came in some grand flash. It was a slow, steady realization—one that emerged as I found myself reaching inward. My body could be beaten, my spirit tested, but my soul—my essence—remained intact. And that revelation became my light in the darkness, a flicker of hope when everything else seemed impossible. There are memories that still feel raw, memories that, when I allow myself to visit them, pull me back to those haunting days. The cold grip of fear returns, tightening its hold, reminding me of what it means to be vulnerable. But vulnerability, I have learned, is not a weakness. It is the greatest act of courage.

One of those haunting memories was when I was locked away with a mentally challenged girl and a pregnant woman. I can still see the hopelessness in their eyes, a look of desperation that mirrored my own in ways that made my heart ache. They had become a prisoner of their own body; their mind weighed down by years of abuse—verbal, physical and emotional. Their spirit had been crushed by those who should have protected them. They were told by others what they could and could not be until they no longer believed they could be anything at all. As I watched them, I saw a reflection of myself, of every person who has ever been told they are less, that they are undeserving of love, of freedom, of life

It is difficult to explain what it feels like to witness someone lose their spirit long before their body gives in. Their suffering was not unique—it mirrored the emotional imprisonment that so many people experience, unseen and unnoticed by the world. That realization was a turning point for me. I could not let my spirit be crushed in the same way. I knew then that I could not live in the shadows any longer. I had to rise not just for myself but for every person who has ever been silenced by the voices of those who claim power over them. I had to rise, not just for me, but for all those who could not rise.

When I reflect on my time in prison, I vividly recall the moments when I believed I would never see daylight again. Every night, I would close my eyes and try to imagine a future beyond the concrete walls that confined me. But there were days when imagining wasn't enough when the weight of hopelessness pressed down too heavily. The pain was relentless, the fear overwhelming. In those moments, it would have been so easy to give in, to let the darkness consume me. But I didn't. I couldn't.

What kept me grounded in those moments wasn't just hope—it was faith. Faith that no matter what happened to my body, my spirit belonged to something greater, something eternal. Faith that there was a purpose behind the pain, a reason for the suffering. Faith that no power in this world could take away the core of who I was. It was this faith that carried me through the darkest of times and that sustained me when I had nothing left. My faith became my anchor, keeping me steady when the storms of life threatened to sweep me away.

Resilience, I've learned, is about more than just surviving. It's about staying true to yourself when everything around you is falling apart. It's about holding onto your values, your beliefs, and your identity, even when the world tries to strip them away. In the years since those dark days, I have often been asked how I managed to endure it all. My answer is simple: I didn't do it alone. I was never truly alone.

Even in the midst of unimaginable hardship, there were moments of grace. There was a boy—just a child, really—who offered me a flattened piece of cardboard to sleep on when I had nothing but the cold, hard ground beneath me. That small gesture, that simple act of kindness, meant everything. It reminded me that even in the worst of circumstances, there is always someone who will reach out a hand to help. And that, I believe, is the essence of resilience—a continuous reaching out, both to others and to something greater than ourselves. We are not meant to endure life's trials alone. We are meant to lift each other up, to find strength in the community, and to be a light for others when their own light has dimmed.

But the most difficult part of resilience wasn't surviving prison or enduring torture. It was the moments after. It was the realization that life outside those walls would never be the same. I had changed. The world had changed. And in many ways, my relationships had changed, too. Separation from my husband for a year and a half taught me that some scars remain even when the wounds have closed. There was a time when I believed that having someone by my side was the only way I could be strong. But being separated, left to face the world alone, showed me a different kind of strength—one that I never knew I had.

For so long, I had relied on my husband to be my anchor, my protector. But when we were torn apart by circumstances beyond our control, I had to learn to stand on my own. I had to learn that my strength did not come from anyone else—it came from within me. I didn't need to depend on anyone else except Jesus to find my footing. I didn't need to hide behind anyone to feel safe.

This wasn't a lesson I wanted to learn. It came with pain—deep, searing pain. But looking back now, I realize that it wasn't about what had happened to me. It was about finding the strength to stand on my own to accept that while human relationships are important, they are not the foundation of who I am. My worth, my identity, my sense of self—these things are not dependent on anyone else's validation. They are mine, and mine alone.

There is a certain kind of peace that comes with this realization—the peace that comes from knowing that you are enough. I found that peace not through some grand, life-changing revelation but through small, quiet moments of introspection. Through prayer. Through allowing myself to grieve the loss of what I thought life should be

RESILIENCE

and then embracing what it actually was. In those moments, I discovered a truth that has carried me through every challenge since I am whole. I am enough with Jesus.

The person I have become is not the same person I was before the pain, before the separation, before the loss. I am stronger, yes, but more than that—I am complete. The journey has not been easy. It has been filled with twists and turns, with moments of despair and flashes of hope. But it has brought me here, to this moment, where my story, though filled with suffering, is also filled with love, faith, and the belief that we are all capable of rising from the ashes, just as the Phoenix does.

There is something profound about the image of the Phoenix, rising from the flames of destruction to become something even greater than it was before. In many ways, we are all like the Phoenix. We go through moments of devastation, moments when it feels like everything we have known has been burned to the ground. But from those ashes, we have the opportunity to rise, to rebuild, to become something new.

I did not simply endure the fires of life—I was transformed by them. They did not destroy me; they refined me. I am still here, not because life has been kind, but because I chose to rise. And just as I have risen, I believe that we all have the capacity to rise, no matter how many times we have been knocked down.

Section II: *Moving Forward*

As I prepare to close this chapter, I want to share something that has been close to my heart—an initiative I started to help women like my grandmother, my mom, and, like me, those who have been silenced, oppressed, or forgotten. After my experiences, I knew I could not stand by and watch others suffer in silence. I began working to create safe spaces for women who have endured trauma where they can heal, find their voices, and rebuild their lives.

This initiative, born out of my own pain, has become a beacon of hope for many. But it is not enough for me to stand alone. I encourage you, the reader, to take initiative as well. Each of us, in our own way, can make a difference. Whether through small acts of kindness, like that boy who offered me a piece of cardboard, or through larger efforts to create change, we all have the power to lift others up. We all have the capacity to help others rise.

There will be moments in life when it feels like the weight of the world is pressing down on you when the challenges you face seem insurmountable. In those moments, I want you to remember that resilience isn't about being unbreakable. It's about allowing yourself to break and then finding the strength to put the pieces back together. And you will.

Life is full of challenges, but it is also full of moments of grace. I have seen the worst that humanity has to offer, but I have also seen the best. I have witnessed people give up when they had nothing. I have seen love in places where I thought only darkness existed. I have seen the power of the human spirit to rise above even the most daunting circumstances.

For those of you who, like me, have been displaced, who have had to leave behind everything you know and love—I see you. I understand the pain of being uprooted, of having to start over in a place that feels foreign. But know this: you do belong. Your story, your experience, is valid. It is worth sharing. And it is worth being heard.

To those who have welcomed refugees, who have opened their homes and their hearts to people like me, I want to say thank you. Your kindness matters more than you will ever know. You have been part of someone's healing, part of their journey toward rebuilding their life. Your compassion has created ripples that extend far beyond the initial act of kindness.

To those in positions of power, I ask this: see us. Truly see us. We are not just statistics. We are human beings, with dreams, with families, with hopes for a better future. We didn't choose to leave our homes. We were forced to, by circumstances beyond our control. All we ask is for the opportunity to rebuild, to contribute, and to be given a chance to thrive.

To anyone reading this who is facing their own trials, know this: you are stronger than you know. You have within you the power to overcome whatever life throws your way. It may not feel like it now, but one day, you will look back and see that the very things you thought would break you were the things that made you who you are. Embrace your story with all its messiness, its pain, and its beauty. Because your story is not just yours—it is a testament to the resilience of the human spirit.

This is the final chapter, but it is not the end. This journey of resilience of rising from the ashes is ongoing. For me, for you, for all of us. We are constantly evolving, growing, and rising. I am not the same person I was when I began this journey, and neither will you be. But I hope, in some small way, that this story has touched your heart, has reminded you of your own strength, and has encouraged you to keep moving forward. This may be the end of the book, but it is not the end of the journey. It never is.

Thank You Note

Dear Readers,

Thank you for taking the time to journey through these pages with me. Your willingness to explore these stories, reflect on their lessons, and connect with the voices within, means more than words can express.

This work exists because of hearts like yours—open, compassionate, and eager to make a difference. I hope this book has inspired, challenged, or uplifted you in some way. Your support is a beacon of encouragement, and I am deeply grateful for it.

May we continue to grow together, embracing resilience, empowering others, and creating a better world.

With heartfelt gratitude,
Danny, Idoshe and I

Me and Danny   *Me and Idoshe*

C.G. Women's Empowerment (CGWE)

Dureti (Mimi) Tadesse
Founder & CEO
+1614-441-1020
cgweafrica@gmail.com

Get Involved:

Visit: cgweafrica.com

Give: cgweafrica.com/donate

Follow + Share: @cgweafrica

Dream Big "For nothing is impossible with God" Luke 1:37